# THE GLOBAL CHALLENGE OF AUTISM

## HEARING

BEFORE THE

SUBCOMMITTEE ON AFRICA, GLOBAL HEALTH,
GLOBAL HUMAN RIGHTS, AND INTERNATIONAL
ORGANIZATIONS

OF THE

## COMMITTEE ON FOREIGN AFFAIRS
## HOUSE OF REPRESENTATIVES

ONE HUNDRED THIRTEENTH CONGRESS

SECOND SESSION

———

JULY 24, 2014

———

## Serial No. 113–205

———

Printed for the use of the Committee on Foreign Affairs

Available via the World Wide Web: http://www.foreignaffairs.house.gov/ or
http://www.gpo.gov/fdsys/

———

U.S. GOVERNMENT PRINTING OFFICE

88–833PDF          WASHINGTON : 2014

For sale by the Superintendent of Documents, U.S. Government Printing Office
Internet: bookstore.gpo.gov   Phone: toll free (866) 512–1800; DC area (202) 512–1800
Fax: (202) 512–2104   Mail: Stop IDCC, Washington, DC 20402–0001

## COMMITTEE ON FOREIGN AFFAIRS

EDWARD R. ROYCE, California, *Chairman*

CHRISTOPHER H. SMITH, New Jersey
ILEANA ROS-LEHTINEN, Florida
DANA ROHRABACHER, California
STEVE CHABOT, Ohio
JOE WILSON, South Carolina
MICHAEL T. McCAUL, Texas
TED POE, Texas
MATT SALMON, Arizona
TOM MARINO, Pennsylvania
JEFF DUNCAN, South Carolina
ADAM KINZINGER, Illinois
MO BROOKS, Alabama
TOM COTTON, Arkansas
PAUL COOK, California
GEORGE HOLDING, North Carolina
RANDY K. WEBER SR., Texas
SCOTT PERRY, Pennsylvania
STEVE STOCKMAN, Texas
RON DeSANTIS, Florida
DOUG COLLINS, Georgia
MARK MEADOWS, North Carolina
TED S. YOHO, Florida
SEAN DUFFY, Wisconsin
CURT CLAWSON, Florida

ELIOT L. ENGEL, New York
ENI F.H. FALEOMAVAEGA, American
  Samoa
BRAD SHERMAN, California
GREGORY W. MEEKS, New York
ALBIO SIRES, New Jersey
GERALD E. CONNOLLY, Virginia
THEODORE E. DEUTCH, Florida
BRIAN HIGGINS, New York
KAREN BASS, California
WILLIAM KEATING, Massachusetts
DAVID CICILLINE, Rhode Island
ALAN GRAYSON, Florida
JUAN VARGAS, California
BRADLEY S. SCHNEIDER, Illinois
JOSEPH P. KENNEDY III, Massachusetts
AMI BERA, California
ALAN S. LOWENTHAL, California
GRACE MENG, New York
LOIS FRANKEL, Florida
TULSI GABBARD, Hawaii
JOAQUIN CASTRO, Texas

AMY PORTER, *Chief of Staff*    THOMAS SHEEHY, *Staff Director*
JASON STEINBAUM, *Democratic Staff Director*

————

## SUBCOMMITTEE ON AFRICA, GLOBAL HEALTH, GLOBAL HUMAN RIGHTS, AND INTERNATIONAL ORGANIZATIONS

CHRISTOPHER H. SMITH, New Jersey, *Chairman*

TOM MARINO, Pennsylvania
RANDY K. WEBER SR., Texas
STEVE STOCKMAN, Texas
MARK MEADOWS, North Carolina

KAREN BASS, California
DAVID CICILLINE, Rhode Island
AMI BERA, California

# CONTENTS

# THE GLOBAL CHALLENGE OF AUTISM

### THURSDAY, JULY 24, 2014

House of Representatives,
Subcommittee on Africa, Global Health,
Global Human Rights, and International Organizations,
Committee on Foreign Affairs,
*Washington, DC.*

The subcommittee met, pursuant to notice, at 2 o'clock p.m., in room 2200, Rayburn House Office Building, Hon. Christopher H. Smith (chairman of the subcommittee) presiding.

Mr. Smith. The subcommittee will come to order, and good afternoon to everybody.

The global incidence of autism is steadily increasing. About one in 68 children have been identified with autism spectrum disorder, or ASD, according to estimates from the Centers for Disease Control's Autism and Developmental Disabilities Monitoring Network. ASD is reported to occur in all racial, ethnic and social economic groups, but is almost five times more common among boys, 1 in 42, than among girls, 1 in 189.

Studies in Asia, Europe, and North America have identified individuals with ASD, with an average of about 1 percent of the population. The prevalence of autism in Africa is unknown, but there is no reason to believe that it is any different, it might even be worse, than other parts of the world.

I note parenthetically that Greg Simpkins and I were in Nigeria twice in the last year, but about 10 years ago I was there for a conference on combatting sex trafficking, something I have worked on for many, many years and after the speech, a man came up and said, what are you doing about autism in Nigeria? And I said, well, nothing. And we have become good friends ever since. He has worked with the Autism Society of America ever since. He said there are at least 1 million children in Nigeria who are dealing with autism, it is probably closer to 2 million, and not dealing with it well because they are so resource lacking.

A new study recently found that each case of autism costs $2.4 million over a lifetime, including the expense of special education and lost productivity for their parents. Meanwhile, 85 percent of autistic adults are jobless or underemployed. It is therefore imperative that people with ASD are empowered to be self-sufficient so they can not only earn money to meet their own needs, but they also can utilize their very special talents that they possess to contribute to society at large. This hearing will examine some innovative strategies to achieve that important goal.

SAP, a global software company, is working to rectify this problem. SAP partnered with Thorkil Sonne, CEO and founder of Specialisterne, to develop the highly successful SAP Autism at Work program. Mr. Sonne, with his 17-year-old son Lars, who is autistic, realized that while those with autism might lack the social skills recruiters are looking for, they possess many attributes high on their radar, as well, intelligence and memory, the ability to see patterns, and attention to detail especially on repetitive tasks.

He reasoned that it would be phenomenal if we could use skills like we see among the autism community in software testing, data analysis and quality controls. He says that there is no reason why we should leave these people unemployed when they have so much talent and there are so many vacant jobs in the high-tech sector. SAP and Mr. Sonne will provide further details of their extraordinary program here today.

Theresa Hussman of the Autism Society put it, I think, very well, in work, at school and in the community, people with autism were often faced with segregation, low expectations, impoverished conditions and denial of opportunity that a society committed to civil rights should find unacceptable.

Today, if you are an adult living with autism, you will likely be unemployed or vastly underemployed living well below the poverty line and denied access to affordable housing and so much more.

Pulitzer Prize-winning journalist Ron Suskind will testify in part about the success with his affinity approach. And he points out in his testimony that for every visible deficit, there is an equal and opposing strength. This population is just like the rest of us only less so and more so. The question increasingly is not if these more-so qualities exist, but where.

Autism used to be described as a disorder characterized by delays or abnormal functioning through the age of 3 in social interaction, communication, or restricted, repetitive and stereotyped patterns of behavior, interests and activities. More recently, behavioral scientists describe a range of such behavior, now referred to as autism spectrum disorder, which includes a more high-functioning version known as Asperger syndrome.

It is medically possible to diagnosis somebody with ASD as early as 18 months or even younger, and a reliable diagnosis can be made by the age of 2. However, symptoms might not present themselves until later in life. Those with some form of autism may never be diagnosed at all.

This has led to a debate over famous people, productive people, often considered geniuses, who appear to have symptoms of autism, especially Asperger syndrome. In the April 3, 2003, issue of the New Scientist magazine writer Hazel Muir revealed the debate over whether geniuses like Albert Einstein and Isaac Newton had Asperger syndrome. Simon Baron-Cohen, an autism expert based at Cambridge, and Oxford University, mathematician, Ioan James, speculated that Newton, the noted English physicist and mathematician, exhibited Asperger traits such as hardly speaking, forgetting to eat, and giving scheduled lectures even to an empty room.

Einstein, the German physicist, was said to have obsessively repeated sentences until he was 7 years old and was notoriously confusing as a lecturer. Both were highly productive scientists, perhaps because of the kind of focus ASD produces rather than in spite of it.

On February 2, 2005, a report by Sue Herera of CNBC presented an interview with 2002 Nobel laureate, Vernon L. Smith, in which he spoke in the way which autism has allowed him to excel. "I can switch out and go into a concentrated mode and the world is completely shut out," Smith is quoted as saying. "If I am writing something, nothing else exists." During the interview, Smith who won the Nobel Prize for inventing the field of experimental economics, admitted that he sometimes is not there in social situations. He said that teaching had forced him to become more social, but it was only because he was talking about issues on which he was already focused.

I raise the issue of intelligence and functionality because we too often see people with ASD as victims who must be cared for when the focus their condition produces may only allow them to be highly successful in certain endeavors. When we begin to look at people with ASD in this light, we can better see how they can be enabled to contribute to society. It just requires understanding of their potential as well as their limitations.

Many fields involving mathematics and science would allow for the intense focus exhibited by people with ASD. Think of the fields of analysis, intelligence, actuary science, and the positions requiring what we commonly call number crunching. The ability to analyze data and see patterns most people would not recognize would be invaluable in analytical jobs.

As Nobel laureate Vernon Smith said, his disconnection from social relationships enabled him to think outside the box, as it were, without concern for violating social norms. He found his condition to be an advantage in enabling greater creativity. In our increasingly technical world, people with ASD actually are becoming more valuable, if we can help them overcome social disconnection and allow them to find fields in which what we thought was their disability is actually an advantage.

We hope today's hearing can be instructive in at least initiating change and perspective on what people with ASD can do to help themselves and make a contribution to society as a whole. We must not continue to waste the talents of people who could make their lives and ours much better.

Finally, I would like to welcome an amazing group of individuals who have and are making an historic difference in the lives of people on the spectrum. As Michael Rosanoff of Autism Speaks puts it in his testimony, "Our mission at Autism Speaks is to change the future for all who struggle with autism spectrum disorders." Each of you, on this expert panel, are already doing that, and I thank you as chair of this subcommittee.

I would like to now yield to my friend and colleague, chairman of the Cybersecurity, Infrastructure Protection, and Security Technologies Subcommittee of the Committee on Homeland Security, Pat Meehan from Pennsylvania.

Mr. MEEHAN. Let me thank you, chairman, and let me thank you for your long association and leadership with this issue, and I think you have so importantly pointed out that this is not just a growing issue here at home, but an issue with global implications.

And while we focus largely on the impact that this has on families and children here in the United States, we appreciate that as we continue to struggle for a better understanding of what may cause autism, a better understanding of what we may be able to do to more effectively assist and treat those who are on the spectrum in different capacities, an appreciation for what may be happening in other parts of the world will be important and vital to our understanding of the kind of information that will help us perhaps make progress, inroads, toward cures and otherwise.

And just as importantly, the attention you are paying to things that are happening around the world but here in this country with what is becoming more and more prevalent, and this is why I am so grateful and intrigued by today's hearing. As we see this dramatic growth in diagnoses and in the number, particularly of boys, that are associated with this, by its very implication, we are seeing more and more who are ageing out of the support services that have been made available by virtue of the state's responsibility to provide an appropriate education.

And we are finding parents who were now dealing with children who are now young adults and beginning to try to transition into a life of adulthood, oftentimes parents in the later part of their lives dealing with huge new struggles. But one of the bright spots has been that with the progress that has been made, we have been able to see the capacity for those with autism at various points on the spectrum to be able to transition effectively into meaningful lives, up to and including meaningful contributions in the workforce, and as you will point out, in some cases, remarkably superior capacities to contribute to the workforce with special skills that they bring.

And I know we will be exploring more of that with the testimony, and I am going to be looking forward to hearing not only the experiences, the positives and the challenges as we look, I think, to continue to address this growing segment which include those who are ageing out of the support systems and will now be looking to begin a life of independence.

We need to be able to look for every opportunity that we can to usher that support along. I thank you for your foresight. I thank you for your leadership on this issue here in the Congress and on behalf of all of those with autism across our Nation.

I am very proud to have the opportunity to be here with you today, and I want to thank you for not only this occasion but holding a hearing on this fundamentally important topic. I am grateful for your leadership on the autism issues, and I am honored to have the chance to highlight some of the great work that is being done by a company, that is a global company, but headquartered in my district in Newtown Square, Pennsylvania.

And it is my privilege to introduce Mr. Jose Velasco. He is the Vice President of Project Management and the head of the Autism at Work Initiative at SAP, Incorporated. Mr. Velasco has held a number of positions since joining SAP in 1998, and before that founded a software company and consulted for Fortune 500 companies. He is also the proud father of two young adults in the autism spectrum. I am delighted to have the honor of introducing him to the members of the subcommittee.

Mr. SMITH. Next on the list is Mr. Thorkil Sonne, who is the founder and chairman of the Specialisterne and Specialist People Foundation with the goal of enabling 1 million jobs for people with autism and similar challenges. He first became involved in autism when his son Lars was diagnosed with infantile autism in 1999. He became active in the Danish Autism Society eventually leaving his position at an IT startup company to establish Specialisterne in 2003. Mr. Sonne is now based in the United States where he is driving the expansion of that Specialisterne model with a goal, as I said in my opening, of enabling 100,000 jobs for people with autism and similar challenges.

We will then hear from Ms. Theresa Hussman, who is a board member of the Autism Society and a director of the Hussman Institute for Autism, a research institute established to improve the lives of individuals with autism and their families. She is also the project coordinator for the Hussman Foundation in this capacity. She conducts the review and processing of grants, coordinates and attends status meetings on existing and potential grants and partnerships, and represents the foundation at charitable events. Ms. Hussman is a parent of a young adult son with autism, and in 2013 was appointed as an advisory member of the Howard County Transition Council for Youth with Disabilities.

We will then hear from Mr. Michael Rosanoff who is a member of the Autism Speaks science team and manages the organization's epidemiology and public health research projects focused on understanding the prevalence and the causes of autism. Since joining the organization in 2007, he has been part of the development team of the Global Autism Public Health Initiative, an effort designed to increase awareness of autism and improve access to services through the collection of public health data and training of providers worldwide. Mr. Rosanoff is also a member of Autism Speaks' grants division, helping oversee the organizations grants giving process for autism research which has committed over $200 million to date.

We will then hear from Mr. Ron Suskind, who is a Pulitzer Prize-winning American journalist and best-selling author. He was the senior national affairs writer for the Wall Street Journal from 1993 to 2000 and has published many books, and most recently his memoir, ''Life Animated: A Story of Sidekicks, Heroes and Autism,'' which explores his own son's own struggle with autism.

Since the book's publication, Ron has traveled the country as an autism expert speaking to audiences at the United Nations, the NIH, University of Chicago and Harvard and, of course, the House of Representatives. He is currently senior fellow at the Center for Ethics at Harvard University.

So if all of you could please come and provide your testimony.

## STATEMENT OF MR. JOSE H. VELASCO, VICE PRESIDENT OF PRODUCT MANAGEMENT AND HEAD OF AUTISM AT WORK INITIATIVE, SAP

Mr. VELASCO. Mr. Chairman, members of the subcommittee, I submit a copy of my written statement for the record, if you allow me to summarize it.

Mr. SMITH. Sure. Without objection, all of your longer versions and any materials you would like to be made are part of the record is so ordered.

Mr. VELASCO. Thank you. SAP would like to thank you for your leadership and for providing us the opportunity to share our views on autism and its global impact.

My name is Jose Velasco. I am head of the SAP Autism at Work initiative in the United States. As you may know, SAP is a global leader in enterprise software with more than 67,000 employees providing business solutions for over 250,000 customers in more than 130 countries.

SAP systems are at the core of large parts of global IT, powering more than 65 percent of the transactions that make up the world's gross domestic product, or GDP. With the current estimate of 1 in 68 children affected by autism, and estimated unemployment rate of 70 to 80 percent and an annual cost to the United States in the range of $175 billion to $196 billion, SAP recognizes the magnitude of the emotional and financial impact that autism has in communities around the world.

SAP also recognizes that there is a real opportunity to leverage the skills of people with autism in the workplace, specifically based on our experience in the technology sector where some of the skills traditionally found in people with autism have a strong affinity with the capabilities needed by companies in our line of business.

SAP also believes that the cornerstone element of innovation is the diversity and perspectives of those who participate in the creative process, including those with autism. In support of these views and in support of SAP's mission to help run the world better and improve people's lives, SAP, in partnership with Specialisterne, announced in May 2013 the inception of the global Autism at Work initiative, a unique effort to train people with autism worldwide with the purpose of providing meaningful and rewarding employment opportunities in core functions of our company such as software development, software testing, customer support, and internal IT functions at SAP, among other positions.

SAP's objective is that by the year 2020, 1 percent of its workforce will be represented by people in the autism spectrum, roughly, 650 positions based on SAP's current global workforce of about 65,000 employees. Since this announcement, SAP has successfully implemented pilot programs in India, Ireland, Germany, Canada, and the United States and is in the early planning stages of a pilot program in Brazil.

SAP is also evaluating the implementation of pilot programs in other locations that may include China, France, Bulgaria, and South Africa. It is expected that at the end of 2014, SAP will count approximately 55 colleagues with autism worldwide, and that by the end of 2015 the number will increase to more than 150.

SAP has executed this vision globally with Specialisterne and locally in the United States in cooperation with Department of Rehabilitation of the State of California, the Office of Vocational Rehabilitation of the State of Pennsylvania, and their service providers ExpandAbility and the Arc of Philadelphia. SAP has leveraged the strength of its partners to create a new, simple, and sustainable process to accommodate our new colleagues. Processes such as nontraditional interviewing methods, preemployment training, on-the-job coaching and SAP personnel autism awareness training.

Chairman Smith, the ultimate goal of diversity and the Autism at Work program is to provide and attract the best possible talent to our company no matter what this talent looks like. We hire our new colleagues in spite of autism. As in spite of the challenges associated with this condition, these new colleagues have arrived at our door, displaying resiliency, loyalty, dedication and, most importantly, a burning desire to work.

We also hire people because of autism, as we are able to leverage the innate abilities oftentimes associated with the condition, including a gifted memory; a natural ability to recognize patterns and deviations in systems or data, which is very much in scope for us; and the ability to concentrate and persevere on tasks over a long period of time while remaining attentive to the smallest details.

We have a long journey ahead of us with many things to discover, but we feel confident that with the help of our partners we will be able to continue to leverage the talents and skills of people with autism. We also feel very confident that soon more companies will have similar programs. SAP has been approached by more than 15 companies interested in understanding how our program was conceptualized and implemented.

On behalf of SAP's diversity and inclusion office, our new colleagues with autism mainly, and on behalf of the SAP employees who have made this initiative possible, we would like to thank you once more for this opportunity to share our experience.

On behalf of the many families like mine who are touched by autism, thank you for your leadership and for your attention. I would be more than happy to take any questions that you may have.

Mr. SMITH. Mr. Velasco, thank you very much for your testimony and your leadership.

[The prepared statement of Mr. Velasco follows:]

TESTIMONY OF JOSE H. VELASCO

HEAD OF AUTISM AT WORK INITIATIVE IN THE UNITED STATES

SAP

HEARING ON

**The Global Autism Challenge**

Before the Subcommittee on Africa, Global Health, Global Human Rights, and International Organizations

Committee on Foreign Affairs

United States House of Representatives

July 24, 2014

### Introduction

Chairman Smith, Ranking Member Bass and Members of the Subcommittee:

SAP would like to thank you for your leadership and for providing us the opportunity to share our views on autism and its global impact.

My name is Jose Velasco; I am responsible for the Autism at Work Initiative in the United States for SAP. SAP is a global leader in enterprise software with more than 67,000 employees providing business solutions for over 250,000 customers in more than 130 countries. SAP systems are at the core of large parts of global IT, powering more than 65% of the transactions that make up the world's gross domestic product (GDP).

Today I would like to share with you the SAP Autism at Work Initiative which in partnership with Specialisterne was launched globally in 2013 with the purpose of providing meaningful and rewarding employment opportunities for people in the autism spectrum in core areas of our business.

### The Autism Challenge

It is estimated that 1 in 168 individuals is affected with Autism Spectrum Disorders (ASD) globally. These numbers are suspected to be higher as the ability to diagnose and address autism varies from country to country.

In the United States, according to the Centers for Disease Control, about 1 in 68 children is affected by Autism Spectrum Disorders. Autism affects boys more often than girls, with about 1 in 42 boys and about 1 in 189 girls.

According to a recent study carried out by the University of Pennsylvania, The London School of Economics and the Children's Hospital of Philadelphia, the lifetime cost of an

individual with autism with an intellectual disability averages $2.4 million while the cost of a person with autism and without an intellectual disability approaches in average $1.4 million. These costs go beyond education and therapy encompassing lost productivity of caregivers among other factors.

It is estimated that the total annual cost to the United States to care for those with autism is in the range of $175 billion to $196 billion; depending on the percentage of people with autism considered to have an intellectual disability (40% and 60% are figures that are typically estimated).

Various other studies point to an unemployment rate in the range of 70% to 80%.

## A Potential Opportunity

While the autism problem is significant and pervasive, reaching every corner of the world, SAP believes that there is a real opportunity to leverage the skills of people with autism in the workplace.

With one of the worst turnover rates of any industry, high tech could benefit from recruiting skilled employees who stay the course, as replacement costs in our industry can reach levels as high as 150% of the annual salary of a person being replaced.

According to Forbes, there are approximately 100,000 unfulfilled Science, Technology, Engineering and Math (STEM) jobs in the San Francisco Bay and New York areas alone. We at SAP have come across very qualified people who have more than adequate credentials to fill jobs in functions that range from HR to Engineering, but who are also in the autism spectrum, and for that reason have not been able to secure a job, often times unable to get past the first interview.

People with autism represent a significant source of talent in both vocational and professional areas. For employers to tap into this talent pool, it would be important to re-think talent acquisition processes that range from interview methods to retention practices.

## The SAP Autism at Work Initiative

In support of these views and in support of SAP's mission to help the world run better and improve people's lives, SAP in Partnership with Specialisterne, announced on May 21, 2013 the inception of the Global Autism at Work Initiative, a unique effort to train people with autism worldwide for employment into core functions of the company, including but not limited to software development and testing. SAP's objective is that by the year 2020, 1% of its workforce will be represented by people in the autism spectrum, roughly 650 positions, based on SAP's current global workforce of over 65,000 employees.

The Autism at Work Initiative is a fundamental paradigm shift on how SAP hires and retains the best possible talent. SAP is bending existing processes and creating new ones as needed to accommodate the employment of people in the autism spectrum.

Since this announcement, SAP has successfully implemented pilot programs in India, Ireland, Germany, Canada, the United States, and is in the early planning stages of a pilot program in Brazil. SAP is currently evaluating the implementation of Autism at Work pilot programs in other locations that may include China, France, Bulgaria and South Africa.

The purpose of these pilots is to distill learnings from various locations resulting in the creation of global processes templates accommodating the local reality of places where we hire colleagues with autism. It is expected that by the end of 2014 SAP will count with approximately 55 colleagues with autism worldwide, and that by 2015 that number will increase to more than 150.

SAP's expectation is that by the year 2020, the company will reach onboarding equivalency in those locations where people with autism are hired. This means that the effort of hiring a person with autism will be little different than hiring anyone else.

An additional important objective of this initiative of SAP for this initiative is to share the experiences we have gained through this pilot with other companies and to hopefully inspire them to start their own autism at work initiatives.

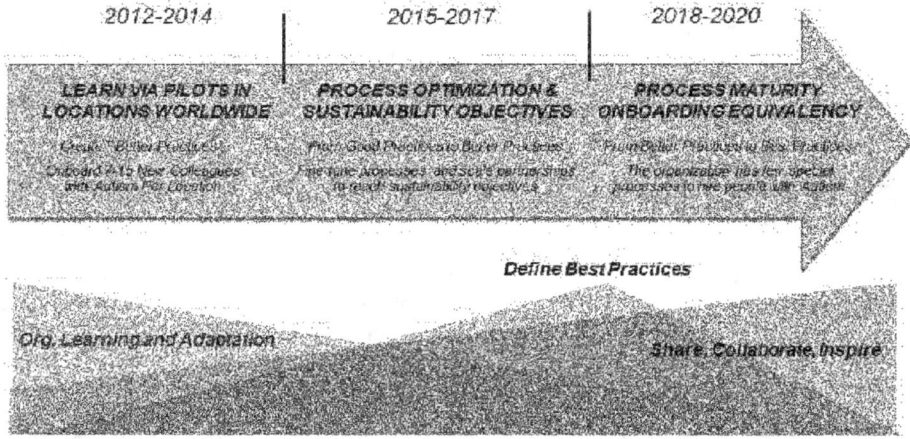

SAP Autism at Work Roadmap

**SAP's Motivation**

There is a rationale behind our efforts to employ people with autism at SAP. We at SAP firmly believe that a cornerstone element of innovation is the diversity of those who participate in the creative process and the perspectives they bring to the table. The relentless pace of innovation in the high tech industry is of key importance as obsolescence and irrelevancy can happen in very short time cycles.

Alan Kay, a renowned computer scientist, fellow of the American Academy of Arts and Sciences and the National Academy of Engineering, once said that a different perspective is

worth 80 IQ points. SAP believes in capturing the perspectives of those who look at the world differently, as it is only through those eyes that we will be able to invent richer and more rewarding solutions for our customers.

There is also a significant body of research that points to the affinity of people in the autism spectrum to science and arts. Hans Asperger, Viennese pediatrician after whom Asperger's syndrome was named once said: "It seems that for success in science or art a dash of autism is essential. For success, the necessary ingredients may be an ability to turn away from the everyday world, from the simple practical, an ability to rethink a subject with originality so as to create in new untrodden ways, with all abilities canalized into the one specialty".

According to Prof. Simon Baron-Cohen, a strong supporter of SAP's Autism at Work and head of the Autism Research Center at Cambridge University in the United Kingdom, there is strong evidence, under current accepted criteria, that Isaac Newton and Albert Einstein, among many luminaries, were in the autism spectrum. Albert Einstein had no friends in childhood, was late to speak, and when he spoke, he did so with echolalia, where he repeated back what he heard. These traits exhibited by Albert Einstein are all consistent with people in the autistic spectrum. Other personalities in the autism spectrum include Susan Boyle, winner of Britain's Got Talent, actors Daryl Hanna and Dan Aykroyd, as well as professor and author Dr. Temple Grandin.

While not everyone in the autism spectrum has the skills and abilities of some of these famous personalities, it is not uncommon to find unique talent within our communities who today are unemployed, partially employed or underemployed and who with some training can carry out functions spanning vocational and professional work.

## Workplace Challenges for People with Autism

But while many people in the autism spectrum may have valuable abilities, it is the accompanying set of challenges associated with the condition that prevents them from pursuing and attaining rewarding employment. Among the principal challenges associated with the condition that we find are social interactions and communications. Reading social cues and dealing with ambiguity can be difficult for many people with autism.

Someone in the spectrum may interrupt a colleague at work who is visibly busy as he or she may not be able to read the other person's body language. And if asked "to be transparent", a person with autism may interpret this literally, as someone asking him or her to permit the uninterrupted passage of light through their bodies instead of interpreting the request as asking them to be open, candid or frank.

Some people with autism may also have hyper-sensitivity to sounds or light. As Dr. Stephen Shore, a Professor at Adelphi University who is in the autism spectrum shares: "those down lights in the ceiling feel like I am looking directly into a spotlight, they can be painful". Dr. Shore wears a baseball cap as a means to address his sensitivity to light. A person with

autism may also have other negatively perceived traits such as failure to look at other people in the eye, reduced ability to smile or not being able to offer a strong handshake.

The challenges for people in the autism spectrum start when they first arrive at a job interview, perhaps wearing a baseball cap, perhaps having a weak handshake, perhaps not smiling or not being able to make eye contact. These "interview killers" are the reason why many people who are otherwise qualified to do a job, are deemed not a good fit for an organization.

### In-spite of Autism and because-of Autism

Many people in the spectrum also exhibit narrow interests, rigid routines, low tolerance for mistakes and "fascination with object parts", as children often times observing things like the wheels and pistons of a toy steam locomotive for hours.

These narrow interests, rigid routines and low tolerance for mistakes are also key traits of people who are good in science, technology, engineering and mathematics (STEM). This is where the traits start to blur between ability and disability, and where some innate characteristics of many people in the spectrum can be of high value in the workplace.

As a software company, SAP views the value that our new colleagues with autism bring to the table in two ways: *"in-spite" of autism* and *"because of" autism*.

- *In spite of autism* and the challenges associated with this condition, our new colleagues have arrived at our door displaying resilience, loyalty, dedication and a burning desire to work.

- *Because of autism*, we are able to capture the innate abilities that are often times associated with people in the autism spectrum. These abilities may not all be present in every individual but generally include a gifted memory, a natural ability to recognize patterns and deviations in systems, processes and data and/or the ability to concentrate and persevere on tasks over long periods of time while remaining attentive to very small details. We have also observed a very low tolerance for mistakes, an essential trait in any job but particularly important in technology related jobs.

In general we believe that there is a strong affinity between the natural ways of our colleagues in the spectrum and software development and IT. This affinity exists in great part due to the unambiguous, precise and predictable nature of the type of work we do.

### The Global Autism at Work Initiative Organization

The SAP Autism at Work initiative is spearheaded by the Global Diversity and Inclusion Office of SAP AE. The initiative counts with a global program office as well as country-specific leads.

As each location is faced with different opportunities and challenges, the Autism at Work initiative is a **global** effort with a central governance model, but providing sufficient execution flexibility to accommodate the **local** reality of each location.

## Global and Local Partnerships

Recognizing that SAP as a company is not an expert in autism, a global partnership was established with Specialisterne to implement the autism at work initiative. Specialisterne's experience and tenure in the field of training and procurement of opportunities for people in the spectrum and their employers, has been a great asset in SAP's Autism at Work journey.

Partnerships have also been established locally in the United States with the Department of Rehabilitation of the State of California (DOR) and The Office of Vocational Rehabilitation of the State of Pennsylvania (OVR). SAP has also partnered with The Arc of Philadelphia and Expandability, two non-profit service providers of OVR Pennsylvania and DOR California respectively. Specialisterne, as trusted advisor, has assisted with the implementation oversight of our end-to-end processes.

SAP has a strong partnership with the Ernie Els foundation and has partnered in the past with the Dan Marino Foundation.

SAP has also established partnerships with Universities such as Cambridge University in the United Kingdom, and is in the process of establishing partnerships with Universities in the United States. These partnerships range from academic/research purposes to sourcing programs for talent in the autism spectrum.

## The SAP Autism at Work Training Process in the United States

The SAP Autism at Work initiative in the United States was just kicked off in January 2014. As of May 2014, twelve individuals have been onboarded into permanent positions at SAP Labs in Palo Alto, CA and SAP America in Newtown, Square, PA.

Upon exploring positions in various SAP departments that would be conducive for a pilot program, twelve full-time job opportunities have so far been identified spanning the following roles: software developers and testers, business analysts, technical writers, IT technical support staff, IT project manager and Customer Support associates. Each position has a career ladder at SAP with compensation packages and benefits similar to those of any other colleague in the company in similar positions and seniority.

Position descriptions were provided to DOR and OVR (in California and Pennsylvania respectively), who identified candidates with autism within their client base. These DOR/OVR candidates subsequently participated in a one-day pre-selection event held at SAP with participation of Specialisterne, Expandability and SAP.

This one day pre-selection event replaces traditional interview practices that typically consist of multiple interviews and where interviewer and interviewee seat in opposite sides of a table. SAP now utilizes Specialisterne's methodology consisting of a "Lego Hangout", where candidates are asked to spend a day at SAP "playing" with Lego Mindstorms. Candidates utilize Lego Kits to build robots based on a set of instructions. Throughout the day each candidate is asked to move go to a different area for a short conversation to learn

more about their interests and background. A Pizza lunch is served halfway through the day making this a fun-filled and relaxed event.

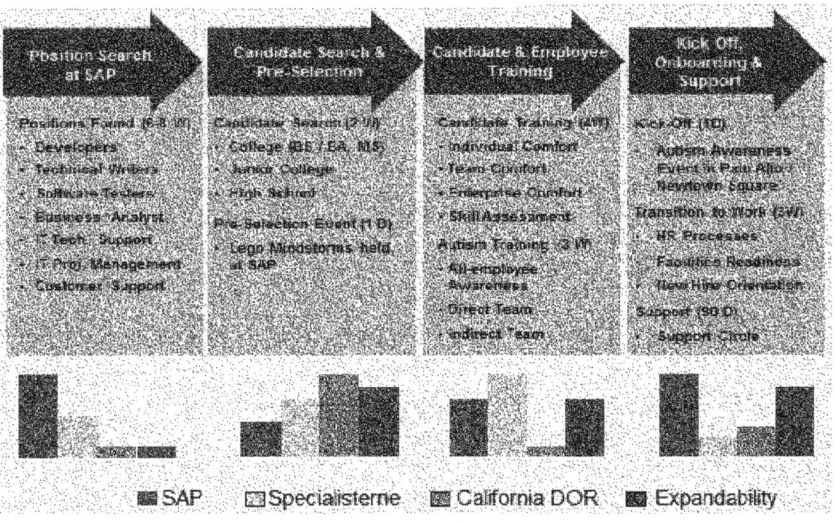

Autism at Work Pilot Program Process implemented in Palo Alto, California.
The Pennsylvania process is similar but delivered via local partnerships with OVR and The Arc.

At the end of the pre-selection event, the candidate list is narrowed down to those who will proceed to the next step in the process: candidate training.

Candidate and personnel training consists of a 4-week program that is funded by DOR and OVR respectively and hosted by SAP. The training was delivered utilizing Specialisterne methodology by the Arc and Expandability.

The main objective behind this training is to provide a soft transition to professional life via specialized modules addressing personal, team and enterprise comfort levels for the new candidates. It is during these four weeks of training that managers and team buddies start getting acquainted with the candidates participating via a number of activities that range from demonstrations to lunches to small assignments provided by the managers. Buddies are team members peers to our new colleagues who will work with them side-by-side.

It is also during this time period that SAP employees and managers are trained. Employees are segmented at a high level in three categories as depicted in the following chart and role-adequate training / support is provided.

| | High-Interaction Employees Colleagues who regularly collaborate with new colleagues with ASD | Medium-Interaction Employees Colleagues who occasionally interact with new colleagues with ASD | Low-Interaction Employees Colleagues with no interaction with new colleagues with ASD | |
|---|---|---|---|---|
| General Autism and AaW Awareness Session | 90 Minutes | 90 Minutes | 90 Minutes | |
| Autism Classroom Training | 1/2 Day | 1/4 Day | | Coaching Need |
| On the Job Coaching (Team &Individual With ASD) | 60-90 Days | | | |

| | | |
|---|---|---|
| · Direct Managers | · Security Staff | · Field Employees |
| · Direct Team Members | · Health Staff | · Sr. Management |
| · HR Business Partners | · Cafeteria Staff | |
| | · Indirect Team Members | |
| | · Recruiters | |

· Intensity of Interaction with ASD-Affected Colleagues
· Function-based specificity of Information needed to Interact with ASD-Affected employees

SAP Autism at Work Pilot Program Employee Training Strategy

### SAP Autism at Work Mentors

It is also during the 4-week training period that a call for volunteers takes place for "Autism at Work Mentors". The Autism at Work Mentors are employees who typically have a strong affinity with the topic of autism, in many cases due to knowing a family member or friend who is in the autism spectrum.

Currently, SAP Autism at Work US has 28 Autism at Work Mentors.

### Backgrounds of our Candidates in the United States

Candidate's educational backgrounds in the United States range from high school to junior college to college. Candidates range in age from early 20's to late 40's. Two female employees are part of the initial group in the United States. Most of our new colleagues were unemployed, partially employed or underemployed prior to joining SAP.

### Post-Onboarding Support in the United States

After candidates finish the 4-week training program and managers have provided approvals for employment to commence, candidates spend the next two+ weeks in administrative tasks filing applications and getting further acquainted with the company among other things.

Once our new colleagues are fully onboarded into their respective teams, a support circle is finalized and implemented.

This support circle consists of six individuals.

- SAP Team Manager
- SAP Team Buddy

- SAP HR Business Partner
- SAP Autism at Work Mentor
- Job Coach from Expandability/The Arc funded by DOR/OVR respectively
- Specialisterne Trainer

Job Coaching and support is provided for the first 60-90 days of employment by Expandability and The Arc. Feedback from managers points to outstanding support delivered by Expandability and The Arc.

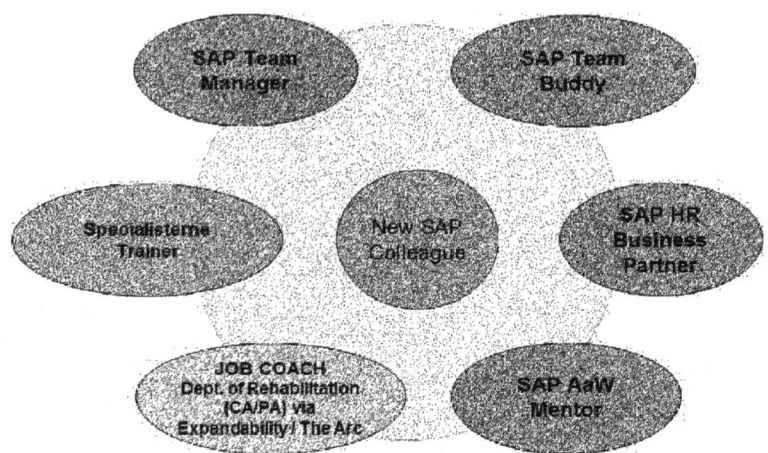

SAP Autism at Work Support Circle

### Life Skills

In some cases, our new colleagues may need assistance with skills that go beyond the work place. These "life skills" include transportation to-and-from work, food preparation, time management, and personal care and leisure activities among others.

Through The Arc and Expandability, our new employees with autism in the United States have benefited from coaching and advice that have allowed them to grow and become more independent.

### Early Results from SAP Autism at Work Pilots

- Early results from our autism pilots indicate that our new employees with autism are integrating well into their teams. Cohesiveness within teams has increased.

- While the processes that have been put in place to train and support our new colleagues and their teams are in a continuous improvement phase, feedback at this time is very encouraging across the board:

  - **Janis Oberman, New Employee** "I am a 56 year old woman who had prior experience in the IT industry. I had been unable to obtain full-time employment since I was laid off in 2001. However, I had kept my skills current though underpaid part-time work and a returned to graduate school. So, I am **thrilled** to get this opportunity to work for SAP as a QA specialist in a Business software development department. Also, the Specialisterne training (with the robots) was phenomenal and I've received more support than I could have hoped for.  I was diagnosed with Asperger Syndrome as an adult, like most people my age, who could not have met the more restrictive criteria for Autism in the 1960's. Additionally, no more SSDI!!! That saves the government $21,959 per year (adjusted for inflation), totaling **$263,508** (for 12 years on SSDI).

  - **Anonymous, New Employee** "SAP has leveled the playing field by recognizing the communication and learning style of those that are on the autism spectrum.  The habits previously seen as quirks are being recognized as a keen ability to pick up detail quickly to benefit our employer, SAP."

  - **Ben Shaibe, Team Buddy** :"Since our new colleague joined our team as a software tester, my day has become brighter, my work more interesting and my feeling of purpose even greater"

  - **Holger Graf, Hiring Manager**: "We are very grateful for the opportunity to be part of this initiative. We have two new colleagues in our team; they are well on their way to being great contributors in the SAP Customer Support Organization"

  - **Gunther Rothermel, SVP** "We can certainly make a lot of progress as society if we dedicate more attention, research and energy to people with special needs, so that we can tap into their talents and abilities"

**Early Recommendations to Other Potential Employers**

- Partnering with Key Entities a key element of SAP's success is the establishment of partnerships with non-profit and state/local government organizations.

- Executive Sponsorship and Grass-Roots Support: without these two elements it is difficult to implement a program.

- Crawl, Walk, Run: plan a multi-year approach. SAP recommends that companies carry out a pilot or pilots to learn, then work on streamlining processes and culture, and lastly, reach scale.

## Outlook

- SAP's mission "to help the world run work better and improve people's lives" continues to be the driver for the SAP Autism at Work Initiative.

- As planned, SAP will move into its process improvement phase in 2015 onboarding additional new colleagues with autism across locations worldwide.

- SAP wishes to inspire other companies to start their own Autism at Work programs and to collaborate to improve the availability of opportunities for people with autism

## Conclusions

Chairman Smith, Ranking Member Bass and Members of the Subcommittee:

The ultimate goal of diversity and the Autism at Work program is for SAP to attract the best possible talent. Companies that consciously look for people considered outliers in the workforce will be able to innovate and succeed.

We have a long journey ahead with many things to discover, but we feel confident that with the help of our partners, we will be able to continue to leverage the talents and abilities that people in the autism spectrum bring to the workplace.

SAP has been approached by more than 15 companies interested in understanding how our program was conceptualized and implemented. Our hope is that we will continue to inspire others to start their own Autism at Work programs and soon have more companies who can share their experiences.

On behalf of SAP's Diversity and Inclusion Office and the employees who have made this initiative possible, we would like to thank you once more for this opportunity to share our experience.

On behalf of many families like mine who are touched by autism, thank you for your leadership.

Thank you for your attention. I would be happy to answer any questions.

Mr. SMITH. I would like to now yield to Mr. Sonne.

## STATEMENT OF MR. THORKIL SONNE, FOUNDER AND CHAIRMAN, SPECIALISTERNE

Mr. SONNE. Thank you, Chairman Smith, for your leadership in this area and thanks for the opportunity to address the global autism challenge here. I have prepared a written statement which I ask to enter into the record.

Mr. SMITH. Yes, without objection, it is part of the record.

Mr. SONNE. Thank you.

So my messages is here, if we take a global job approach to the autism challenge, we can actually unlock a lot of hope, action and impact in the U.S. and globally, and we can create value for all the stakeholders in our society.

My background is as a father of a young man with autism, as a social entrepreneur, as a businessman, and as a former chair of a local branch of Autism Denmark. I founded Specialisterne 10 years ago to train, assess, educate and employ people with autism, and I am happy to be an American resident now since August of last year, to lead the activities in the U.S.

Parents whose sons or daughters have autism are, in my eyes, part of a global family. That goes beyond borders, culture, economy, tradition. We share very much the same destiny. We have gone through the same emotions, and I have been contacted by parents of kids with autism in about 90 countries, and they have asked me to help make a change in their nation and when parents with autism make contact with me, I cannot say no. I can say, be patient. We will find a way. We will get there.

Many families are stuck in their own struggle of concern, despair, and fights. All are driven of the fear of what will happen to our loved ones when we are not their to fight their battles anymore. As long as the parents are able, we will fight the battles, but at some point in time, we won't have these resources anymore. But what if we can give these families a hope that there will be jobs. There will be employers who will respect that people are different and appreciate that talent comes in different shapes.

What if employers are willing to accommodate a working environment where the individual can excel even if they have autism? Well, today you heard from a great example of such an employer, SAP. So I think the question is, how can we as a global family, as global stakeholders, help companies like SAP who want to get access to talented people with autism around the world?

I founded Specialisterne as a social enterprise, to solve a social challenge with a business model. We now have 10 years experience in unfolding talent among people with autism and put these talents to good use when we can match the individual's comfort zone with the work zone. The goal is 1 million jobs, 100,000 in the U.S., another 100,000 in Africa. What we learn in the U.S. through partnerships with businesses, with NGOs that work with people with disabilities, we need to bring to Africa and all continents.

In Africa, in particular, we need to empower the families. We need to give them hope. We need to help go from hope to action through social entrepreneurship and to provide a model for impact where big business, academia, governments, and the education system can work together to create jobs. I see social entrepreneurship as a great tool and a great resource in Africa.

There are 350 social entrepreneurs in Africa supported by Ashoka which select social entrepreneurs with potential to change the local environment in which they act. I am an Ashoka fellow. I am also a Schwab Foundation Social Entrepreneur. They have conferences on Africa. They are connected with the World Economic Forum. When we can connect these stakeholders then we can help release the parent power, turn that into social entrepreneurship that can work with big business and with governments and other stakeholders.

Just imagine if we can invest in creating jobs for people with autism and assist the education system to identify and support differently-abled students with autism in the U.S., Africa, and globally. With a job creation approach to the global autism challenge, we can really make results that will make a lot of sense from a family, a health, a human rights, a business and a financial perspective.

Thanks again for your leadership in this, and I will be happy to answer any questions.

Mr. SMITH. Thank you very much for your leadership as a pioneer and that vision of 1 million jobs, 100,000 in the U.S., couldn't come at a better time. Like Victor Hugo once said, nothing is as compelling as an idea whose time has come. So thank you for your pioneering work.

[The prepared statement of Mr. Sonne follows:]

**SPECIALISTERNE**
Passion for details

TESTIMONY OF THORKIL SONNE

FOUNDER AND CHAIRMAN

SPECIALISTERNE AND SPECIALIST PEOPLE FOUNDATION

HEARING ON

## The Global Autism Challenge

Before the United States House of Representatives

Committee on Foreign Affairs

Subcommittee on Africa, Global Health, Global Human Rights, and International Organizations

July 24, 2014

## Introduction

Thank you, Chairman Smith, Ranking Member Bass and Members of the Subcommittee.

I appreciate the opportunity to be here today to share my view on the global autism challenge. With the growing prevalence of autism and growing costs for care we need to work together to improve the opportunities for individuals affected by autism becoming active and welcomed members of the societies in which they live.

I am grateful for your leadership, Mr. Chairman, on this important issue and for addressing the autism challenge in a global perspective.

My background for discussing the global autism challenge is as a father to a child with autism, as active member in autism organizations, as a business professional and as a social entrepreneur.

In particular I will address my experience in working with SAP, represented by Mr. Jose Velasco, on selecting, training and on boarding individuals with autism in high tech jobs.

## Autism

Autism (autism spectrum disorder) is a complex developmental disability that typically appears during the first three years of life and affects a person's ability to communicate and interact with others. Autism is defined by a certain set of behaviors and is a "spectrum disorder" that affects individuals differently and to varying degrees. There is no known single cause of autism.

SPECIALISTERNE
Passion for details

Some of the behaviors associated with autism include delayed learning of language; difficulty making eye contact or holding a conversation; difficulty with executive functioning, which relates to reasoning and planning; narrow, intense interests; poor motor skills' and sensory sensitivities. A person on the spectrum might follow many of these behaviors or just a few, or many others besides. The diagnosis of autism spectrum disorder is applied based on analysis of all behaviors and their severity. *(Source: Autism Society of America)*

**Autism prevalence in the US**

In March 2014, the Center for Disease Control and Prevention issued an autism prevalence report which concluded that the prevalence of autism had risen to 1 in every 68 births in the United States. By the age of eight 46% of children diagnosed with autism in America have normal or above normal intelligence.

In June 2014, researchers from University of Pennsylvania estimated the lifetime cost related to an individual with autism with intellectual disability to average $2.4 million and $1.4 million related to an individual with autism without intellectual disability. The costs to the US society related to adults with autism in the US is estimated to be between $175 billion and $196 billion per year. A large part of the costs relates to loss of productivity.

**Autism globally**

Epidemiological data estimate the global prevalence of autism to be one person in 160. This prevalence estimate represents an average figure, and reported prevalence varies substantially across studies. Some well-controlled studies have, however, reported rates that are substantially higher. The prevalence of autism in many low- and middle-income countries is as yet unknown.

The prevalence of autism appears to be increasing around the world. There are many possible explanations for this apparent increase in prevalence, including improved awareness, expansion of diagnostic criteria, better diagnostic tools and improved reporting.

Most individuals with autism and other developmental disorders live in low- and middle-income countries; however, most of the knowledge about these conditions is based on research done in high-income countries.

Worldwide, individuals with autism and other developmental disorders represent a vulnerable group. They are often subject to stigma, discrimination and human rights violations, including unjust deprivation of health, education and social opportunities. Globally, access to services and support for individuals with developmental disorders is inadequate, and families of those affected often carry substantial emotional and economic burdens.

Autism was brought to the attention of Member States and the United Nations General Assembly in January 2008, when the General Assembly adopted resolution A/RES/62/139 designating 2 April each year as World Autism Awareness Day. The subsequent observation of that day has substantially increased international awareness about autism. *(Source "Autism spectrum disorders & other developmental disorders - From raising awareness to building capacity" World Health Organization)*

**SPECIALISTERNE**
Passion for details

## Autism in Africa

Autism research conducted in Africa has been infrequent and unrepresentative of all African countries, making the prevalence of autism in Africa difficult to estimate. There is a substantial lack of psychiatrists with knowledge on autism.

Examples for Sub Sahara countries from International Association for Child & Adolescent Psychiatry & Allied Professions (IACAPAP) show:

• Liberia has one adult psychiatrist serving populations of 3.4 million respectively

• Gambia's population of 1.7 million people is served by two expatriate psychiatrists on a short term contract

• Nigeria has one adult psychiatrist serving the needs of over one million

• Ghana has one adult psychiatrist serving the needs of over one million people

Accurate national autism statistics in South Africa are hard to come by but with just 9 specifically tailored schools in the entire country, an estimated 135 000 autistic children are not getting the specialized education they need. *(The South African Medical Journey)*

## Families

Very often families who have one or more members with autism are constrained in their ability to understand and train the individual with autism to prepare for active participation in society. Individuals with autism risk being bullied in school, dropping out of the education system and being rejected by employers due to challenges in social interaction. The challenges do not only concern the individuals with autism but the whole family where parents often have to reduce their participation in the labor force in order to take care of their family members with autism.

The ultimate goal for most families is for the family member with autism to achieve a meaningful and productive job and through the job establish a fruitful and independent life situation.

Few families have the resources themselves to create better opportunities for their family member so they seek to organize their own efforts through autism organizations. However – when resourceful parents have the right conditions to make a change the impact can be amazing, making a positive change in society. I have seen a huge power in the grass roots of parents with family members with autism.

If we can empower families to understand and train their family members and to advocate for or start initiatives within education and employment we can tap into the power of the grass roots and improve the opportunities for individuals with autism around the globe.

## Education

Education opportunities are often inadequate and costly for society and/or families. The success of including students with autism in a traditional class room very much depends on well-educated and compassionate teachers.

A large part of individuals with autism who succeed to graduate from higher education will face a major challenge in meeting recruiters and qualify for jobs. The labor market expects

social skills in addition to professional skills and employers very often lack the understanding and accommodation needed to take advantage of the skillsets of individuals with autism.

My experience tells me that transition from education system into the labor market is one of the biggest challenges for individuals for autism. The labor market requires strong social skills for most jobs and the recruitment meeting often turns into a bad experience for individuals with autism as they are measured according to a social skills paradigm. The stigma in the labor market is huge and we need to form common ground between the individuals comfort zone and the work zone.

To lower the barriers from the education system into the labor market internships are great tools by which individuals with autism and managers will have a longer period of time to ensure that the individual with autism will have a fair opportunity to excel and demonstrate value for the company.

### Autism seen as untapped talent pool

Individuals with autism often finds their self-esteem in the work they do. As such a job is of utmost importance for the individual to establish a positive life situation.

In particular the high tech sector can benefit from skill sets often related to autism like a good memory, attention to detail, structured way of working, ability to perform repetitive jobs with high accuracy and innovation. Examples of tasks like quality control, analysis, data entries and logistics can be found in several business areas.

Despite the potential talents and the attractiveness for the labor market it is expected that up to 70% of adults with autism are unemployed or under employed according to Autism Society of America.

The inability for societies to provide and thereby develop the talent among individuals with autism combined with the inability for the labor market to make use of the talent is a major global challenge that calls for action.

### Social entrepreneurship

A social entrepreneur is an individual who develops an innovative business model to solve a social challenge. Social entrepreneurs are mostly people who have a deep insight in a social challenge and a strong motivation to make a substantial change in society to eliminate the challenge. Amazing changes are carried out across the world by social entrepreneurs who often are supported by global organizations like Ashoka Innovators for the Public and Schwab Foundation for Social Entrepreneurs (who are affiliated with the World Economic Forum). A number of Ashoka Fellows work on education and employment of individuals with autism and other disabilities across the world.

Social entrepreneurs have the innovation and flexibility to find solutions in their local community and to partner with stakeholders to scale the solution and make a substantial change.

**SPECIALISTERNE**
Passion for details

### The Specialisterne experience

When my youngest son was diagnosed with autism in 1999 I learned about the challenges for a family to prepare a member with autism for a meaningful and productive life situation as adult. A combination of family drive, experiences from being chairman of a local branch of Autism Denmark and a position as technical director in an IT company made me challenge society by claiming that stakeholders in our society should work together to include individuals with autism and similar challenges in the labor market.

As an attempt to remove the divide between talented individuals with autism and the need for talent in the labor market I founded Specialisterne (The Specialists) in Denmark in 2003 as a social enterprise. The ambition is to assess, train and employ individuals with autism based on understanding and accommodation. Specialisterne has for more than 10 years been working with the local government to train and educate adolescents and adults with autism and with the corporate sector to provide services where individuals with autism can provide competitive tasks within coding, quality control, analysis, data entries and logistics.

Specialisterne has expanded to 12 countries. In 2013 I relocated with my family to the US to lead the activities in the US with the aim to enable 100,000 jobs for individuals with autism within 10 years through partnerships and knowledge share. Specialisterne US is a non-profit organization operating in DE, NY, PA, CA and ND. We have partnered with companies like SAP and CAI and NGOs like The Arc and ExpandAbility to match talented individuals with autism with corresponding jobs.

Working with Specialisterne for more than 10 years I have seen how individuals with autism have unfolded talent and brought it to good use in meaningful and productive jobs. I have seen what it means to quality of life when individuals with autism are appreciated and respected for the work they do. I have met many parents who feel relieved by the new independent life situation for a family member with autism.

In addition I have seen employers been taken by surprise by the skillsets of individuals with autism and puzzled by how individuals with a disability can be able to perform as good as or better than non-disabled employees. Besides appreciating the professional skills of the new colleague managers among corporate partners have told me how they have grown as managers from working with new colleagues with autism. The value based management style is based on respect, accommodation, clarity and accessibility has turned out to have a positive impact on the work climate in the department where the new colleague works.

In order to lower the barriers between education and jobs we established Specialisterne Youth Education to work with the transition of adolescents with autism into an active adulthood. We have experienced the importance of working with students to improve life skills and to bring them into internships among corporate partners.

SPECIALISTERNE
Passion for details

## Experiences from addressing the global autism challenge

Since I founded Specialisterne I have been contacted by families with members with autism from 90+ countries with requests to bring education and employment opportunities to their community.

In order to respond to these requests I founded the non-profit Specialist People Foundation with the goal to enable one million jobs for people with autism and similar challenges throughout the word.

In 2006 I had the opportunity to speak at the World Autism Congress in South Africa. Through listening to testimonies and interacting with participants I learned about the vulnerable situation for most families with members with autism in Africa. Through my work with WHO, Ashoka and World Economic Forum I have met people working with the autism challenge in countries like Egypt, Morocco, Nigeria, Ghana, Lesotho and South Africa.

My impression is that the lack of understanding of autism in Africa is pervasive with South Africa as an exception. It will take decades before adequate capacity in identification, care and education for individuals with autism.

## Experiences from partnership with SAP to create jobs globally

SAP announced May 2013 that it will work globally with Specialisterne to employ people with autism as software testers, programmers and data quality assurance specialists. SAP sees a potential competitive advantage to leveraging the unique talents of people with autism, while also helping them to secure meaningful employment. By 2020 1% of the SAP global work force will be represented by individuals with autism through the Autism at Work program. In the partnership SAP has so far employed individuals with autism at SAP locations in India, Germany, Ireland, Canada and USA.

This year I have worked with SAP, the Philadelphia Chapter of The Arc, Office of Vocational Rehabilitation Pennsylvania, ExpandAbility and Department of Rehabilitation California to search, select, train and on board individuals with autism through the Specialisterne model in Newtown Square and Palo Alto. SAP has been very dedicated to combine the work zone with the comfort zone of the new colleagues. As an example an internal and external support organization has been established to ensure that the new colleagues will feel welcome and be given the best possible opportunities to excel. With this support structure in mind we are not just talking about jobs but start of careers.

The experience of working with SAP has been very successful and has generated a lot of interest from companies across the US. Thanks to SAP's position as a global role model I foresee a large number of national and global partnership with leading companies which will create jobs and become role models not just in the US, but globally.

Mr. Jose Velasco, SAP, will in his testimony give an insight in the background, motivation and experiences of SAP.

**SPECIALISTERNE**
Passion for details

## Conclusion

Chairman Smith, Ranking Member Bass, Distinguished Members of the Subcommittee:

With all this in mind, permit me to conclude by citing UN Secretary-General Ban Ki-Moon from the UN World Autism Awareness Day Message 2013:

> *"Autism is not limited to a single region or a country; it is a worldwide challenge that requires global action. This international attention is essential to address stigma, lack of awareness and inadequate support structures. Now is the time to work for a more inclusive society, highlight the talents of affected people and ensure opportunities for them to realize their potential."*

The corporate sector has the capacity to act as a role model for employment of individuals with autism in the US, globally and in particular in societies with low awareness about autism as in Africa. In particular global companies have the advantage of bringing experiences from employing individuals with autism in the Western World to Africa.

As drivers in job creation, corporate companies and social entrepreneurs should be encouraged to work together to find the best way to develop the talents of individuals with autism globally and locally. Social entrepreneurs will be well positioned to work with other stakeholders like families, NGO's, local governments and education providers to facilitate assessment, training and education which will reduce the barriers between individuals with autism and employers.

My experiences from Specialisterne and partnerships with companies like SAP and CAI gives me hope that we can make a difference in dealing with the global autism challenge.

We can deal with the global autism challenge by

- helping families with members with autism to become advocates for change and provide support to establish schools and small businesses through social entrepreneurship
- providing knowledge on autism and education services from the rich world to the medium and low income world through virtual platform for any family and school with access to the internet
- encouraging global companies to work as role models in job creation and facilitate partnership with social entrepreneurs and NGOs
- developing a platform for match making between individuals with autism and jobs
- encouraging academic partnerships by which universities can document and disseminate best practices

Mr. Chairman, Committee members

The vision of Specialisterne is a world where people are given equal opportunities in the labor market and the goal is to enable one million jobs for people with autism and similar challenges.

We can get far by taking a partnership based job creation approach to deal with the global challenge of autism.

I thank you for your attention and will be happy to answer questions.

---

Mr. SMITH. Ms. Hussman.

## STATEMENT OF MS. THERESA HUSSMAN, BOARD MEMBER, AUTISM SOCIETY

Ms. HUSSMAN. Congressman Smith and members of the committee, it is my pleasure and honor to be asked to appear before you and to talk about what we believe is the most critical and important need for over 3 million individuals who have an autism diagnosis.

My name is Theresa Hussman, and I am a dedicated volunteer of the Autism Society of America, the Nation's oldest and largest grassroots national autism organization. Our organization's president, Scott Badesch, is currently hosting 1,000 people at our national conference in Indianapolis, and he asked me to come and present the testimony for him.

With over 105 affiliates serving close to 1 million people each year, the Autism Society national network works each day to improve the quality of life for all who live with autism. We do this in ways that are outcome-based, and I am proud that we are fully inclusive having individuals with autism, family members, professionals and community leaders in all parts of our governing and advisory boards.

In addition to serving with the Autism Society of America, my husband John and I are the very proud parents of four young adults, one of whom has autism. Over the past decade, we have been among the largest private funders of autism research and recently established the Hussman Institute for Autism, a research institute founded on the principles that people with autism have far more competence than they may be able to demonstrate or that society allows them to achieve. I want to commend this subcommittee, and especially the leadership of Chris Smith, for holding this important hearing.

A few years ago, there was a video that went viral of a young man with autism named Jason McElwain, they called him "J-Mac." He spent his high school years as a manager of his high school basketball team because he had a passion for the game. In his senior year, he was allowed to play 4 minutes and 19 seconds of a game. During that time he made 7 baskets, 6 points of which were 3-pointers. While millions who watched celebrated that brief moment of opportunity, those of us who advocate for our loved ones with autism also asked why wasn't he on the court the whole year?

In school, at work and in the community, people with autism are often faced with segregation, low expectations, impoverished conditions and denial of opportunities that a society committed to civil rights should find completely unacceptable. Today, if you are an adult living with autism, you will likely be unemployed or vastly underemployed, living well below the poverty line and denied access to affordable housing and much more.

The most agreed-upon rate of unemployment or underemployment among adults with autism is close to 70 percent. Think for a minute, if any other group of individuals in our Nation had such a high rate of unemployment. While companies are now starting to move in the right direction to address this dire statistic, including SAP, AMC Theaters, Walgreens, UPS, EMS Insurance and many more, the reality is that behind each of those statistics is the lack of our Nation's attention to fully integrate those living with autism into our mainstream society.

Though universal access is often expected of our buildings and of our stairways, our society has yet to build that universal access into our schools, our curricula, our workplaces, our hearts, and our minds. A person living with autism has every right to be included in the mainstream of society, but it isn't occurring.

Ask almost any parent of a school-aged child with autism about their struggles with public school systems, and they will tell you story after story about lack of inclusion, denial of rights, and inadequate educational supports. You will hear about schools that underestimate children with autism and limit their educational opportunities. While we watch the number of children diagnosed on the autism spectrum increase, we fail to prepare these educators, paraprofessionals and school administrators to properly support their students with autism. Yet, every one of them will come across a child on the spectrum every day.

Many school districts and superintendents fight against laws that would regulate the harmful impact of restraints and seclusion on innocent students with autism. Even though research has demonstrated that these approaches are entirely unnecessary when people with autism are provided with appropriate, positive behavioral support.

Many colleges define their commitment to educational opportunities for a person with a disability as being little more than some extra time to take a test. It is rare to find a school leader who is held accountable by his or her governing board for the success of students with disability. Autism creates enough barriers for individuals to demonstrate their ability and to engage with their community. We need our Nation to lower those barriers in every aspect of life, not to build them higher.

With respect to employment, too many public schools and colleges are not addressing the educational and job skill development needs of our students with autism, leaving adults with autism untrained or unprepared for employment. Fortunately, many employers are now beginning to advance their hiring of autistic adults, and they demonstrate that if given a chance, an adult with autism will be an outstanding employee.

Oftentimes, the Federal Government reinforces the perception that individuals with autism and for that matter any developmental disability can't work in meaningful jobs. In the State of the Union address, President Obama suggested a $10.10 minimum wage for workers paid through Federal grants and contracts. But it is so common to underestimate and marginalize workers with a disability that they weren't originally part of this effort. Fortunately, many organizations including the Autism Society advocated for inclusion of individuals with a disability in that Executive order, and we are proud that the President assured inclusion of workers with a disability.

At the Autism Society, we believe that educational inclusion, employment opportunities, and equal participation in community life are civil rights. As in other civil rights struggles, our Nation needs the moral conscience to embrace people with autism as different, not as less. The answers are not difficult. First, we must ensure that every government agency and body respects the value and dignity of each person living with autism, or for that matter, any disability. Secondly, we must assure that if a government entity is helping all people, it does so in a way that is inclusive of those with autism.

We must also ensure that people educational institutions are held accountable for seeing that students with a disability are provided the same level of educational opportunities as those without a disability. We know that those few educational institutions that do provide a high commitment to opportunity for students with a disability are showing that with support, a student with a disability can be successful.

A strong example is Marshall University in West Virginia, and Evan Badesch, who is the son of our organization's president. With proper support and Evan's amazing desire and commitment to obtaining a quality education, he is succeeding. This is because the university, from its wonderful President Dr. Stephen Kopp to all of the faculty, are fully committed to ensuring that every student, regardless of their condition, can succeed. They see the value of such success and they know it is the right thing to do.

The Autism Society believes that we also must change the national discussion regarding autism from simply cause and cure to one of hope, acceptance, support, and opportunity. We can seek to improve the lives of people with autism without sending the message that they are not yet enough to be loved, valued, and accepted as they are.

Finally, and we believe this is critical, we must focus our efforts through a private/public partnership that does not rely on Government to do it all. I again, want to commend Congressman Smith who is working with us in addressing adult services in a way that assures maximum opportunities by advancing proven best practices through a public/private effort. People with autism deserve more than 4 minutes of the game. Real change that embraces them in the mainstream of our society will only come when we all work together.

I thank you for your very important attention to this critical matter, and I would be happy to answer any questions.

Mr. SMITH. Ms. Hussman, thank you very much for your testimony and for the perspective that you bring to this.

[The prepared statement of Ms. Hussman follows:]

**Testimony by**
**Theresa Hussman**
**Volunteer**

Autism Society of America
4340 East West Highway
Suite 350
Bethesda, MD

Subcommittee on Africa, Global Health, Global Human Rights, and International Organizations

Thursday, July 24, 2014 at 2:00 p.m.

Congressman Smith and members of the Committee...

It is my pleasure and honor to be asked to appear before you and to talk about what I believe is the most critical and important need for the over 3,000,000 individuals who have an autism diagnosis. My name is Theresa Hussman and I am a dedicated volunteer of the Autism Society of America, the nation's oldest and largest grassroots national autism organization.  Our organization's president, Scott Badesch couldn't be here today since he is with over 1000 individuals attending our 45th annual Autism Society national conference in Indianapolis today.

With over 105 affiliates serving close to a 1,000,000 people each year, the Autism Society national network works each day to improve the quality of life for all who live with autism.  We do this in ways that are outcome based and I am proud that we are fully inclusive, having individuals with autism, family members, professionals and community leaders in all parts of our governing and advisory boards. In addition to serving as a volunteer with the Autism Society of America, my husband, John and I are the very proud parents of four young adults, one of who has autism.  Over the past decade we have been among the largest private funders of autism research and recently established the Hussman Institute for Autism, a research institute founded on the principle that people with autism have far more competence than they may be able to demonstrate or that society allows them to achieve.

I want to commend this committee, and especially the leadership of its Chairman Chris Smith for holding this important hearing.

A few years ago there was a video that went viral of a young man with autism named Jason McElwain who spent his high school years as the manager of his school basketball team, because of his passion for the game.  In the last home game of his senior year, he was allowed to play during the last 4 minutes and 19 seconds, in which time he made 7 baskets, six of them as 3 pointers. While millions who watched celebrated that brief moment of opportunity, those of us who advocate for our loved ones with autism also asked why wasn't he on the court the whole season?

In school, at work and in the community, people with autism are often faced with segregation, low expectations, impoverished conditions and denial of opportunity that a society committed to civil rights should find unacceptable.

Today, if you are an adult living with autism, you will likely be unemployed or vastly under-employed, living well below the poverty level, and denied access to affordable housing and so much more.  The most agreed-upon rate of unemployment or under-employment among adults with autism is close to

70%. Imagine for a minute if any other group of individuals had such a high rate of unemployment. While companies are now starting to move in the right direction to address this dire statistic including SAP, AMC Theaters, Walgreens, UPS, EMC Insurance and many more, the reality is that behind each of these statistics is the lack of our nation's attention to fully integrate those living with autism into the mainstream of society. Though universal access is often expected of buildings and stairways, our society has yet to build universal access into schools, curricula, workplaces, our hearts, or our minds.

A person living with autism has every right to be included in the mainstream of society. But, it isn't occurring. Ask almost any parent of a school age child with autism about their struggles with public school systems and they will tell you story after story about lack of inclusion, denial of rights, and inadequate educational supports. You will hear about schools that underestimate children with autism and limit their educational opportunities. While we watch the number of children diagnosed on the autism spectrum increase, we fail to prepare educators, paraprofessionals, and school administrators to properly support those students with autism. Yet every one of these professionals will come into contact with a student on the spectrum.

Many school districts and superintendents fight against laws that would regulate the harmful impact of restraints and seclusion on innocent students with autism, even though research has demonstrated that these approaches are entirely unnecessary when people with autism are provided with appropriate, positive behavioral support. Many colleges define their commitment to educational opportunities for a person with a disability as being little more than some extra time to take a test. It is rare to find a school leader who is held accountable by his or her governing board for the success of students with disabilities. Autism creates enough barriers for individuals to demonstrate their ability and to engage with their community. We need our nation to lower those barriers in every aspect of life, not to build them higher.

With respect to employment, too many public school systems and colleges are not addressing the educational and job skill development needs of students with autism, leaving adults with autism untrained or unprepared for employment. Fortunately, many employers are now beginning to advance their hiring of autistic adults, and they demonstrate that if given a chance, an adult with autism will be an outstanding employee.

Often times, the federal government reinforces the perception that individuals with autism, and for that matter any developmental disability, can't work in meaningful jobs. In his State of the Union address, President Obama suggested a $10.10 minimum wage for workers paid for through federal grants and contracts. But it is so common to underestimate and marginalize workers with a disability, that they weren't originally part of this effort. Fortunately, many organizations, including the Autism Society advocated for inclusion of individuals with a disability in that executive order, and we are proud that the President finally assured inclusion of workers with a disability. Congress still also allows sub-minimal wages paid to individuals with a developmental disability in certain instances, based on archaic and inaccurate perceptions of what a person with a disability can and can't do.

At the Autism Society we believe that educational inclusion, employment opportunities, and equal participation in community life are civil rights. As in other civil rights struggles, our nation needs the moral conscience to embrace people with autism as different, and not less.

The answers are not difficult. First, we must ensure that every government agency and body respects the value and dignity of each person living with autism, or for that matter any disability. Second, we must ensure that if a government entity is charged with helping all people, it does so in a way that is inclusive of those with autism. We must also ensure that public educational institutions are held accountable for seeing that students with a disability are provided the same level of educational opportunities as those without a disability. We know that those few educational institutions that do provide a high commitment to opportunity for students with a disability are showing that with support, a student with a disability can and will be a true success story.

A strong example is Marshall University, where Evan Badesch, the son of our organization's president attends. With proper support and Evan's amazing desire and commitment to obtaining a quality education, he is succeeding. That is because the university, from their wonderful president Dr. Stephen Kopp to all their faculty, are fully committed to ensuring that every student, regardless of their condition, can succeed. They see the value of such success and they know it is the right thing to do.

The Autism Society believes that we also must change the national discussion regarding autism from simply cause and cure to one of hope, acceptance, support, and opportunity. We can seek to improve the lives of people with autism without sending the message that they are not yet enough to be loved, valued, and accepted as they are.

Finally, and we believe this is critical, we must focus our efforts through a private/public partnership that does not rely on government to do it all. I again want to commend congressman smith who is working with us in addressing adult services in a way that assures maximum opportunities by advancing proven, best practices through a public/private effort. People with autism deserve more than four minutes of the game. Real change that embraces them into the mainstream of our society will only come when we all work together.

I thank you for your very important attention to this critical issue and I would be happy to answer any questions.

---

Mr. SMITH. And the long advocacy of Autism Society of America, I have been involved since 1980, and I will never forget when we had a game-changing moment in my district in Brick where we thought there was a prevalence spike, and I introduced the bill called the Assure Act, which is really the Combating Autism Act, it is almost identical with some tweaks. And CDC and NIH were against it and thought it was a solution in search of a problem.

I will never forget it. It was, you know, really difficult to understand the lack of interest given the example CDC spent $287,000 per year on their entire program. I mean, that doesn't buy a desk and one or two people. And I often ask them, what do you do? It took 3 years to get the bill passed. It was title I of the Children's Health Act.

And the reason why I mentioned it, the Autism Society was instrumental throughout that whole process gaining cosponsors and educating and educating and educating members who, again, many of whom at the time, typically in 1997, 1998, shared the view that this was extraordinarily rare, 3 in 10,000 was the number when I got elected, and a lot of us clung to that as, well, that must be the number. So thank you for that longstanding leadership.

Mr. Rosanoff, I am going to recognize you in a moment but there is a vote on, a couple votes. We will take a recess. And several members have said they wanted to be here and they will come, I am sure. But this is, I think, an opportunity to round them up. Thank you. We will stand in brief recess.

[Recess.]

Mr. SMITH. The subcommittee will reconvene and continue with this hearing.

And I recognize Mr. Rosanoff.

### STATEMENT OF MR. MICHAEL ROSANOFF, ASSOCIATE DIRECTOR, PUBLIC HEALTH RESEARCH, AUTISM SPEAKS

Mr. ROSANOFF. Thank you.

Chairman Smith, Ranking Member Bass, members of the subcommittee, thank you for the opportunity to share Autism Speaks experience working with autism communities around the globe.

My name is Michael Rosanoff. I am the associate director of public health research at Autism Speaks. Since 2007, I have managed the organization's epidemiology research portfolio, research focused particularly on measuring the prevalence and economic cost of autism in the U.S. and worldwide. I am also a member of the organization's international scientific development team helping lead Autism Speaks' Global Autism Public Health Initiative, currently active in over 50 countries around the world.

I am formally trained in public health and epidemiology and have a personal family connection to autism. Our mission at Autism Speaks is to change the future for all who struggle with autism spectrum disorders. This can mean funding scientific research for those families struggling to understand the causes of autism; it can mean developing strategies to help those struggling to overcome barriers that limit access to effective services; or it can mean providing support for those struggling to receive acceptance and opportunities to contribute to society.

Because autism knows no ethnic, cultural, or geographic boundaries, neither does Autism Speaks. In 2007, the United Nations adopted a resolution recognizing April 2 as an annual day of world autism awareness. In response to the increase in awareness worldwide and with it the increase demand for information and support, Autism Speaks launched the Global Autism Public Health Initiative in 2008, with the objective to develop sustainable, broad-reaching and culturally-sensitive programs that build local capacity for autism research and service delivery. This is accomplished through multidirectional knowledge transfer and multinational collaboration among diverse stakeholders.

In just over 5 years, our international team has traveled more than 1 million miles and spoken with hundreds of affected individuals, parents, professionals, and government officials. Today, I would like to offer you some of our experiences and important lessons learned.

The autism community is diverse, with a diverse set of challenges and a diverse set of strengths. As autism is a lifelong condition, those challenges and strengths often change over the course of time, thus, there is no single one-size-fits-all solution to improving lives of those touched by autism. Autism is not simply a health issue but also an educational issue, a social welfare issue, and a human rights issue. The most effective strategies are those that are comprehensive and multi-sectorial.

For example, in developing a national strategy for autism in Bangladesh, the government established an inter-ministerial task force to implement a coordinated plan of action across eight government ministries, including health and education, also social welfare, labor, and even finance because to achieve a truly inclusive society, autism is as much a labor and finance issue to increase employment opportunities as it is an education issue to achieve inclusive education.

Across countries, while cultures, belief systems, public health infrastructure, and resources may differ, all families around the world want the same for their loved ones with autism: Improved awareness to reduce stigma; statistics to know they are not alone; to advocate for policies, increased access to evidence-based services earlier in life and throughout life; and more opportunities for individuals with autism to reach their fullest potential in life and society, especially after their caregivers are gone.

Common goals mean that common approaches can be effective across diverse settings which makes cross-country collaboration and idea sharing so important. Approaches do, however, need to be tailor-fit to different country contexts. What may be an effective strategy in one may not be feasible in another. Strategies must be adapted to fit the environment while maintaining their active ingredients.

Today, the most practical and effective approach to increasing autism support is through community-based programs. The purpose of these programs is to relieve some of the demand placed on the few highly-trained professionals in clinical settings by transferring skills and knowledge to members of the community such as health workers, teachers, and parents.

To help create a package of care that is transferable, especially in low-resource settings, Autism Speaks has teamed up with the World Health Organization in developing the intervention guide and training program to the delivery of autism services by community health workers in nonspecialized settings.

The model is currently being used in Ethiopia as part of a project funded by Autism Speaks and as a result of the initial success of the program, the Ministry of Health of Ethiopia has made autism and mental health in general national priorities. They are currently organizing a conference on the scaling up of mental health services in the country. The WHO and Autism Speaks are also exploring models for parent training and the delivery of autism interventions.

These activities with the WHO were among those identified as priorities as part of an international consultation on autism. The first of its kind meeting in the history of the WHO took place in Geneva last September. More than 75 representatives from nearly 50 different international organizations participated, and among the most discussed and highly-prioritized issues were community inclusion and adult employment. This comes as no surprise considering that based on current best estimates of autism prevalence, every year tens of thousands of children with autism become adults with autism. How are we preparing them for society and is there adequate opportunity for them to pursue employment and independent or assisted living?

In Geneva, we heard about innovative models for identifying unique talents of individuals with autism that would make them valuable assets to an employer. Two of those models came from Specialisterne and SAP, both of whom you have heard from today. But there is nothing like seeing the success of models firsthand, models of community inclusion and practice.

In Bangladesh I visited a center for individuals with disabilities in a small, rural community on the outskirts of the capital city Dhaka. The community itself surrounding the center was unlike any I had seen before. Well, it looked like other roads I had seen elsewhere in Bangladesh with small shops and markets selling clothing and groceries. The difference was that individuals with disabilities including intellectual disabilities and autism staffed all the shops. Not only were these individuals learning employable skills such as counting money at the register, but they were bringing money into their community and, most importantly, raising awareness of disabilities.

I also had the great fortune to travel to Lima to visit the Centro Ann Sullivan de Peru, or CASP. CASP is a center for individuals with different abilities, not disabilities. It first opened its doors over 30 years ago in a garage and now has hundreds of current students and past graduates. The curriculum is community based, where 30 percent of services are delivered at CASP, and 70 percent are delivered at home in real-world settings.

Students learn real-world tasks needed to survive in a city environment such as using mass transportation. That is a skill they will need to be able to get to and from a job. A goal for all students at CASP is to get a job. That is not just true for those with autism who are less severely affected. Even those with greater challenges often have or can learn skills that are attractive to employers and these individuals can be successful in a career with the right support.

Importantly, the staff at CASP works with members of the community such as the bus drivers and employers to educate them about autism which in turn perpetuates a more inclusive society. In a resource-poor country like Peru, it is not uncommon for graduates of CASP to actually become the family breadwinners, earning enough money to help support the entire family. Why couldn't this model work elsewhere?

This brings me to a lesson learned: We must not overlook that knowledge transfer goes both ways. We can learn as much as we can teach, if not more by working with autism communities from around the world. Countries and regions with limited resources and professional capacity had been for years developing innovative solutions to overcome the gap in autism services and the challenges to community inclusion that we experience even here in the United States.

In just the last few years, the pace of development for autism has accelerated rapidly and globally. A new United Nations General Assembly resolution adopted in December 2012 increased the commitment and accountability of governments worldwide to address the social and economic challenges of autism. And following the WHO consultation, the World Health Assembly adopted a resolution that provides a framework for the enhancement of national health systems to include autism services.

Many countries have since developed national autism action plans and passed autism legislation. For example, in Africa, the country of South Africa for the first time has a framework for mental health including developmental disabilities and autism. And earlier this year, 14 African nations participated in an autism Congress sponsored by Autism Speaks in Ghana, where the First Lady of Ghana and the Minister of Health in Tanzania committed to enacting change for the autism communities of their countries.

Worldwide, governments are listening and the commitment is there; however, know-how and capacity are often not. The final lesson learned I would like to share today is that legislation does not necessarily translate into action. Many of the autism laws passed in recent months around the world are well-intentioned but lack the strategy and resources to implement properly. In some cases, poor execution leads to unsuccessful programs that may actually hurt the chances for future support. More concerning is that hope can turn to helplessness for members of the autism community under these conditions.

In India, there have been inclusive education laws in effect for many years, yet true school inclusion has not been achieved. I just returned last week from a consultation in New Delhi with the World Bank working with the disabilities and education communities to develop and improve strategy for inclusive education in India.

It is clear that you cannot simply put children with autism into a classroom without properly training the teacher and educating the students. Furthermore, in a place like India, you cannot simply train a teacher only on autism where there are many other children with other disabilities that also have a right to inclusion. It is important that we consider working with and learning from other disability advocates as we aim for acceptance and inclusion for our loved ones with autism.

Autism is a highly prevalent and highly costly condition to societies around the world. At least 1 in 68 children in the U.S. has an autism spectrum disorder, and research suggests that prevalence may be the same or higher elsewhere around the world. A recent study estimated that the costs to U.S. society are $236 billion per year, with much of that cost due to adult residential care and loss of productivity for both caregivers and adults with autism, many of whom could be earning greater income.

The time to act is now, and there are already models available that are improving access to services and promoting community inclusion around the world. By working together and learning from one another, we can change the future for all who struggle with autism worldwide.

Thank you for your time, and thank you to the many families, professionals and government officials who have welcomed Autism Speaks to their countries to learn from their experiences.

Mr. SMITH. Mr. Rosanoff, thank you very much for your testimony.

[The prepared statement of Mr. Rosanoff follows:]

AUTISM SPEAKS
It's time to listen.

## THE GLOBAL CHALLENGE OF AUTISM

### TESTIMONY PRESENTED TO THE HOUSE COMMITTEE ON FOREIGN AFFAIRS, SUBCOMMITTEE ON AFRICA, GLOBAL HEALTH, GLOBAL HUMAN RIGHTS, AND INTERNATIONAL ORGANIZATIONS

### BY MICHAEL ROSANOFF, ASSOCIATE DIRECTOR, PUBLIC HEALTH RESEARCH, AUTISM SPEAKS

### JULY 24, 2014

Chairman Smith, Ranking Member Bass, members of the subcommittee, thank you for the opportunity to share Autism Speaks' experience working with autism communities around the globe.

My name is Michael Rosanoff, and I am the Associate Director of Public Health Research at Autism Speaks. Since 2007, I have managed the organization's epidemiology research portfolio, particularly research focused on measuring the prevalence and economic costs of autism in the United States and worldwide. I am also a member of the international scientific development team, helping lead Autism Speaks Global Autism Public Health Initiative, currently active in over 50 countries around the world. I am formally trained in public health and epidemiology, and have a personal family connection to autism.

Our mission at Autism Speaks is change the future for all who struggle with autism spectrum disorders. This can mean funding scientific research for those families struggling to understand the causes of autism. It can mean developing strategies to help those struggling to overcome barriers that limit access to effective services. Or it can mean providing support for those struggling to receive acceptance and opportunities to contribute to society.

Because autism knows no ethnic, cultural, or geographic boundaries, neither does Autism Speaks. In 2007, the United Nations adopted a resolution recognizing April 2nd as an annual day of World Autism Awareness. In response to the increase in awareness worldwide, and with it the increased demand for information and support, Autism Speaks launched the Global Autism Public Health Initiative in 2008. The objective: to develop sustainable, broad-reaching, and culturally sensitive programs that build local capacity for autism research and service delivery. This is accomplished through multi-directional knowledge transfer and multi-national collaboration among diverse stakeholder groups.

In just over five years our international team has traveled more than one million miles and spoken with hundreds of affected individuals, parents, professionals, and government officials. Today I would like to offer you some of our experiences and important lessons learned.

The autism community is diverse, with a diverse set of challenges *and* a diverse set of strengths. As autism is a lifelong condition, those challenges and strengths often change over the course of time. Thus, there is no single one-size-fits-all solution to improving lives of those touched by autism. Autism is not simply a health issue, but also an education issue, a social welfare issue, and a human rights issue. The most effective strategies are those that are comprehensive and multi-sectorial. For example, in developing a national strategy for autism in Bangladesh, the government established an inter-ministerial taskforce to implement a coordinated plan of action across eight government Ministries including Health, Education, Social Welfare, Labor, and even Finance. Because to achieve a truly inclusive society, autism is as much a Labor and Finance issue to increase employment opportunities, as it is an education issue to achieve inclusive classrooms.

Across countries, while cultures, belief systems, public health infrastructure, and resources may differ, all families around the world want the same for their loved ones with autism. Improved awareness to reduce stigma, statistics to know they are not alone and to advocate for policies, increased access to evidence-based services earlier in life and throughout life, and more opportunities for individuals with autism to reach their fullest potential in life and society, especially after their caregivers are gone. Common goals mean that common approaches can be effective across diverse settings, which makes cross-country collaboration and idea sharing so important.

Approaches do, however, need to be tailor fit to different country contexts. What may be an effective strategy in one country may simply not be feasible in another. Strategies must be adapted to fit the environment while maintaining their active ingredients. Today, the most practical and effective approach to increasing autism support is through community-based programs. The purpose of these programs is to relieve some of the demand placed on the few highly trained professionals in clinical settings, by transferring skills and knowledge to members of the community such as health workers, teachers, and parents.

To help create a package of care that is transferrable especially in low resource settings, Autism Speaks has teamed up with the World Health Organization (WHO) in developing an intervention guide and training program for the delivery of autism services by community health workers in non-specialized settings. This model is currently being used in Ethiopia as part of a project funded by Autism Speaks. As a result of the initial success of this program, the Ministry of Health of Ethiopia has made autism and mental health in general, national priorities. They are currently organizing a conference on the scaling-up of mental health services in the country. The WHO and Autism Speaks are also exploring models for parent training in the delivery of autism interventions. In fact, my colleague was in Geneva just this week for a working group on this topic.

These activities with the WHO were among those identified as priorities as part of an international consultation on autism spectrum disorders and other developmental disabilities.

The first of its kind meeting in the history of the WHO took place in Geneva last September. More than 75 representatives from nearly 50 different international organizations participated. Among the most discussed and highly prioritized issues were community inclusion and adult employment. This comes as no surprise considering that based on current best estimates of autism prevalence, every year, tens of thousands of children with autism become adults with autism. How are we preparing them for society and is there adequate opportunity for them to pursue employment and independent or assisted living?

In Geneva, we heard about innovative models for identifying unique talents of individuals with autism that would make them a valuable asset to an employer. Two of those models come from Specialisterne and SAP, both of whom you will hear from today. But there is nothing like seeing successful models of community inclusion in practice. In Bangladesh, I visited a center for individuals with disabilities in a small rural community on the outskirts of the capital city Dhaka. The community itself, surrounding the center, was one unlike any I had seen before. It looked like other roads I had seen elsewhere in Bangladesh with small shops and markets selling clothing and groceries. The difference was that individuals with disabilities, including intellectual disabilities and autism, staffed all of the shops. Not only were these individuals learning employable skills such as counting money at the register, but they were also bringing money into the community and, most importantly, raising awareness of disabilities.

I also had the great fortune to travel to Lima to visit the Centro Ann Sullivan de Peru, or CASP. CASP is a center for individuals with different abilities – not disabilities. It first opened its doors over 30 years ago in a garage and now has hundreds of current students and past graduates. The curriculum is community-based where 30% of services are delivered at CASP and 70% are delivered at home and in real-world settings. Students learn real-world tasks needed to survive in a city environment such as using mass transportation. That is a skill they will need to be able to get to and from a job. A goal for all of their students is to get a job. This is not just true for those with autism who are less severely affected. Even those with greater challenges often have or can learn skills that are attractive to employers. And these individuals can be successful in a career with the right support. Importantly, the staff at CASP works with members of the community, such as bus drivers and employers, to educate them about autism which in turn perpetuates a more inclusive society. In a resource poor country like Peru, it is not uncommon for graduates of CASP to actually become the family breadwinners, earning enough money to help support the entire family. Why couldn't this model work elsewhere?

This brings me to another lesson learned. We must not overlook that knowledge transfer goes both ways. We can learn as much as we can teach, if not more by working with autism communities from around the world. Countries and regions with limited resources and professional capacity have been for years developing innovative solutions to overcome the gap in autism services, and the challenges to community inclusion, that we experience even here in the United States.

In just the last few years the pace of development for autism has accelerated rapidly and globally. A new United Nations General Assembly resolution adopted in December of 2012 increased the commitment and accountability of governments worldwide to address the social and economic challenges of autism. And following the WHO consultation, the World Health

Assembly adopted a resolution that provides a framework for the enhancement of national health systems to include autism services. Many countries have since developed national autism action plans and passed autism legislation. For example, in Africa, the country of South Africa for the first time has a framework for mental health including developmental disabilities and autism. Earlier this year, 14 African nations participated in an autism congress sponsored by Autism Speaks in Ghana, where the First Lady of Ghana and the Minister of Health of Tanzania committed to enacting change for the autism communities of their countries.

Worldwide, governments are listening and the commitment is there. However the knowhow and capacity are often not. The final lesson learned I would like to share today is that legislation does not necessarily translate into action. Many of the autism laws passed in recent months around the world are well-intentioned but lack the strategy and resources to implement properly. In some cases, poor execution leads to unsuccessful programs that may actually hurt the chances for future support. More concerning is that hope can turn to helplessness for members of the autism community under these conditions.

In India, there have been inclusive education laws in effect for many years, yet true school inclusion has not been achieved. I just returned last week from a consultation in New Delhi with the World Bank, working with the disabilities and education communities to develop an improved strategy for inclusive education in India. It is clear that you cannot simply put children with autism into a classroom without properly training the teacher and educating the students. Furthermore, in a place like India, you cannot simply train a teacher only on autism when there are many children with other disabilities that also have a right to inclusion. It is important that we consider working with and learning from other disability advocates as we aim for acceptance and inclusion for our loved ones with autism.

Autism is a highly prevalent and highly costly condition to societies around the world. At least 1 in 68 children in the U.S. has an autism spectrum disorder and research suggests that prevalence may be the same or higher elsewhere around the world. A recent study estimated that autism costs U.S. society $236B per year with much of the cost due to adult residential care and loss of productivity for caregivers and adults with autism, many of whom could be earning greater income.

The time to act is now and there are already models available that are improving access to services and promoting community inclusion around the world. By working together, and learning from one another, we *can* change the future for all who struggle with autism worldwide. Thank you for your time, and thank you to the many families, professionals, and government officials who have welcomed Autism Speaks to their countries to learn from their experiences.

Mr. SMITH. We are joined by Chaka Fattah from the Appropriations Committee and with whom I have worked for years on a number of issues especially with respect to brain health.

Mr. FATTAH. Well thank you, Mr. Chairman. Let me thank the panel.

I am not a member of the subcommittee, but the chairman and I have worked together on a number of important issues including safe blood in Africa, which has been credited with helping millions that live and have increased life chances on cord blood, but of late, over these last few years, working on neuroscience or brain-related illnesses, and we have launched legislation to create a global Alzheimer's fund.

But today, we join together, and I am cosponsoring his legislation on autism, and this is some very important work. Now, Ron, in your testimony, you refer to——

Mr. SMITH. He hasn't talked yet.

Mr. FATTAH. Oh, he hasn't talked yet. Okay.

Well, thank you, Mr. Chairman. I will yield. I want to hear his testimony. I will wait until he testifies and then I will ask. Thank you.

Mr. SMITH. We now recognize Pulitzer Prize winner, Ron Suskind. Please proceed.

## STATEMENT OF MR. RON SUSKIND, AUTHOR

Mr. SUSKIND. Thank you, Chairman Smith and all the members that are here today on this busy day. Thank you for giving me an opportunity to speak in a forum like this.

As many of you know, I have been in this town for some decades, usually on the other side of these various tables, walking around with my pad and my tape recorder, writing for the Wall Street Journal, writing six books now. This last book is my sixth, and seeing a town that is often locked in a kind of zero-sum conversation. One person's benefit is another person's loss. Pie is only so big. This is not one of those conversations, which gives me some hope. This is as close to a win-win as you usually get in a town like this.

What we have here is a community that we are now increasingly identifying as folks who can lead their own pass. For every dollar we spend to help them, we know if we look at Thorkil's model, we look what SAP is doing, they will return many dollars in all the ways our economists love in productivity, in independent life, and save extraordinary amounts of money that frankly they don't want us to spend anymore than anyone does.

In a tight Federal budget saying several hundred billion a year is money we do not have. We are at a point of inflection in this debate, which is why I am hopeful. I am hopeful to hear what is being said at the table and what is being said from the dais where elected representatives say, "I get this."

You know, I have been at this for a long time, and I have traveled the world during the last 20 years talking to people who had been left behind, in urban America, in Afghanistan, in Pakistan and what I find with many of them, they are living a life that is context blind. Now, we know that term from our own kids. It is often said that autistic kids are context blind. Well, I say, yes, in some ways they are context deep.

But the context that we reward, the one that is kind of the shared context, picking up queues of knowing who is where and where they sit, what they come to the table with, all that kind of social engagement context. I think we reward that too much, and we will find going forward that we are often better off embracing its counterpoint which is difference, which is the deep well of variance and the deep power of distinction.

You know, many of those kids from Afghanistan and Pakistan, I sit with them. I am like, the kid is unlettered. He is context blind. But he is improvisationally gifted, born of survival, born of the ingenuity that comes from survival and in Southeast Washington, where I reported for years, I found the same thing. I wrote about a kid, the stories that won the Pulitzer Prize. What does he do? He doesn't learn the basic block and tackle of education. His brain, and we know the brain is ever shaping itself, has not been shaped that way. He didn't get that shaping from an education system.

So he is in a tough spot at Brown University, the one guy in a decade from his inner city school here at Ballou High School to make it. He is caught. What does he do? He writes a 68-line epic poem on heterogenous and homogeneous grouping. He has an affinity. This affinity, in terms of poetry and rap music, he finds a way to use that to dissect a complex issue of education.

Now, I want to give that guy a prize and society does, too. What we are seeing is the one-size-fits-all model that rewards some traditional learners, folks who get the game and how it is played. Well, it is discarding too many people in a society that cannot afford to do that. We are throwing away too much human capital, possibility and potential, and the canary in the coal mine, I think, is this population that we are talking about today. Absolutely. They are exactly like us, just extreme versions, all right.

Now, I know we want to say this is a terrible illness and a Holocaust. I felt that. My son is 23. We have been at it for 20 years. And there are times where you say it is a tragedy. But then over time, all of our kids have said, hmm, I wouldn't use that word actually. Because I can do some things. Look what I can do. If you just listen and don't try to make me more like you but help me be more like me in a nourished and supported way, I can show you stuff.

And that is what happened in this story. Traveling the world, talking to the disenfranchised, sitting with them in mud huts, sitting with them, caught in terrible circumstances of violence often borne of bigotry, of violent tribalism. What do I find? 1993, I find the most significantly disenfranchised person I have met is living in the bedroom on the second floor. It is my son.

He is whacked with autism just shy of his third birthday. Chatting away, late onset, they call it. I love you. Let's get ice cream. Where are my Ninja Turtles? At two and then we moved to Washington where I became the senior national affairs writer for the Wall Street Journal. Big moment for the family. On our way up. Everything seemed just right. I was full of certainty and smugness. All working out. My mother was just so proud of me.

And then we got whacked and then Owen started to vanish. Late onset autism, usually between 18 and 36 months. He lost function. First, he wouldn't look at us, then he wouldn't talk to us, then he could not speak. The few-hundred-word, 2½-year-old vocabulary ends up being one word a few months later. And then we heard the first word of regressive autism.

Autism. We didn't know much about it. Now, the chairman talks about pushing forward legislation in 1980. What did the public know of autism in 1980? Well, not very much. But even back then, there was talk of the refrigerator mothers. Well, in 1988, most of our education happens because most of us here saw "Rain Man" with Dustin Hoffman. That is mostly what we knew. Rain Man Babbitt and when we got that diagnosis, we said, there is no way my son is that guy. We embraced denial, which is a powerful force, not one I recognized as powerful as it is back then.

So here is a story as it unfolds. He loses speech. He is alone. The world is talking to him like Charlie Brown's teacher. Wah, wah, wah, wah, wah, wah. Charlie Brown. He can't even hear the Charlie Brown. The one thing, though, that seems to give him comfort, the only thing, is the thing he loved before the onset of the autism, the Disney animated movies. I am like, this can't be. I mean, not Disney. But yes, Disney.

So what we did together as a family is the only thing we could do as a family. Of course, I have an older son, 2½ years older than Owen. We watched the animated movies up in the upstairs bedroom of our Georgetown house not far from here, the only thing that seemed to give him comfort. Now, at this point my son is murmuring gibberish.

At this point, he is talking like baby talk because he has lost speech and he is back to the early antecedents of speech where babies murmur gibberish, and he is saying, "juicervose, juicervose, juicervose." My wife thinks he wants more juice. Doesn't want the juice. But we are upstairs watching a movie called "The Little Mermaid." Anyone here seen that movie? Yeah. Yeah. The chairman has seen it, so I think everyone should raise their hand. We have all seen it. Yeah. Yeah. He has the power of the chairmanship.

And Ariel, you got it. No, you are on it, you know. Which character? Do you think King Triton is kind of your guy? Is that your character? Yeah. I mean, look, I think it works. Yeah.

Mr. Chairman is the sidekick that helps the hero fulfil her destiny; that is not Triton. That is a different character. More Sebastian. Sebastian is good. Watch the movie. He is the one you want to be.

So, we are watching the movie up in the bedroom. It is the part where Ariel, the protagonist, wants to transform herself. To become human this mermaid, she must make a trade with the villain, the sea witch who says, I won't cost you much, a trifle really, just your voice. Owen rewinds. You know, his motor function has collapsed except the rewind button. That's good, he rewinds it again. His brother says Owen, just watch the movie. All of a sudden Cornelia says to me it is not juice. I said what? It's not juice. It's just. Just your voice. I grab Owen, silent for a year, and he looks at me for the first time in a year and says juicervose, juicervose, juicervose. This is our moment. We called it our Helen Keller/Anne Sullivan moment.

Our specialist said don't be so sure. This is called echolalia. They memorize sound. They don't know what the words mean. This is often the way we see this population. If they can't express it, it doesn't exist. They can't show and tell of their emotions, we assume there are no emotions to offer. That is the way we used to think. It is changing. But this is 1994, and our therapist said echolalia. I said is that like what it sounds like? That's right, like a parrot. That is right. We went through several years of this. Several years where he is murmuring lines from movies.

What do we find to make this story come to its crest? We find he memorized 20 Disney animated moves of sound alone, and if you threw him a line, he would throw you back the next line. We spoke in Disney dialogue for years. I mean because everything is in the 50 animated Disney movies and ''Snow White and the Seven Dwarfs.'' I mean what is not in there? So he would just pick a scene. At the beginning it was ''The Jungle Book,'' I am Baloo. I know the height thing doesn't really work but you know I am kind of goofy. My wife is Bagheera, the panther, protective. That worked, that is type casting. His big brother is King Louie, and Owen of course is Mowgli. He throws you a line. You throw him back the next line.

Over years we became animated characters, and this is how he gets his speech back. Took a couple years, but it happened and then, he turns the hundreds of hours of memorized dialogue and lyrics into an emotional language all his own, invented one. Inventing an emotional language. That's something that gets a big bell rung. Then he developed a life philosophy and he writes a story at the end of the book ''Life Animated,'' my book, which is his original story.

Now, what does this tell us? This tells us a profound thing that maybe people know anecdotally at this table and society is learning by the hour, that these affinities, every kid has got one. Often they have several but usually one more than others. They are like life boats for these kids. Over the many decades with autism, the view was wean them off of it. It is perseverative, it is wheel in the ditch, it is obsessive. Definition of obsession, interest to the exclusion of all else. Well, that is the way they are built. They can't dance around like bees going flower to flower. They lock on. They are not foxes. They are hedgehogs.

Again, they are like us, extreme versions of us. This is what we learn against our will. The years we locked the television set because he was doing all-night movie marathons, and we were just going crazy. At times we said let's use it as a behavioral tool. If you want to watch your favorite video, here is ten things you've got to do, each like walking across hot coals. His behavior spiked a little, a little improvement at school but then trailed off. Like we had cut him off from his supply line.

We tried everything until finally my wife in her wisdom says, respect his affinity, enjoy it with him. Look we can't try to fix him every minute. That is not a parent-child relationship, not one that works and then we got in the basement with him, and we danced and we sang and we played characters; and he knew we weren't going to pull the rug out from under him. That is the key because we see these affinities, and they can see we are impatient. And we know they are across the landscape.

Some kids are into Disney. Lots of Disney. I would say the predominant one frankly, but a lot are animated. There is Thomas the

Tank Engine, there are maps, there are train schedules. A parent came to me and said black and white moves from the 40s and 50s. I am like really? How old is he? He is 14. There is a lot to work with there. Get in there with him. Speak 40s black and white movies, speak map, speak Disney.

Here is the key. What they learn and what my son learned in terms of basic education, general knowledge, it was vast. He learned to read by reading credits, again because that is the way he is like is only more so. That is the way we all are. The thing that fires us, our passion, it is always our pathway. It is not even like working. We learn to play the game in schools. Oh, my God. I got to memorize this. When is the test, and I forget it the next morning. These kids are never going to learn that. They are not wired that way. Their reward circuitry doesn't work like that. Their passions are their pathways.

So this is what we learn and then question is what do we do. This is creating change in the community that is in a way overdue and oddly expected. People have been talking about this for years. There is a tipping point we are seeing now. What does it mean in terms of what we can do? Well, what it means is that we now have a clear pathway that Thorkil and the other folks of this committee are seeing as well to say, yes, got it. Exactly like us only more so and less so. All right.

How does that work? Well, the less so part is to make them fit into systems of valuing human ability that we know are kind of one size fits all and don't work very well. Well, what we are doing there is measuring the less sos every day, trying to fix that part and often ignoring the more sos. Again exactly like us. It is the distribution that is the key. What are those more so parts? Hard to measure and why should that surprise you? Faith, will, adrenalin, creativity, the best stuff is hardest to measure.

It is our yardsticks that need to be changed. That is part of the discussion we had during the recess, all of us together. How do we change the yardsticks? What happens when you have got a one size fits all yardstick that some kids succeed by managing and get that slot at Goldman Sachs or McKinsey. What do you do when that yardstick gets gold plated, even when we know it is bent? The mission, of common purpose in this period is to offer a new set of yardsticks that actually reflect the way we are in terms of the diverse character of human beings. Is that going to be difficult? Of course. Is that something government can help with? Absolutely. But those yardsticks are crucial because what happens going forward?

Let me tell you what is happening right now in my crazy little shop up at Harvard. What we are doing is we are gathering affinities. We have folks coming to the LifeAnimated.net Web site. The book is only out 3 months, but there is a kind of energy, a revolutionary pop that is occurring. We say show me that affinity in a video. So we got the videos piling up. Every one like Owen.

Using the affinity, and one of the researchers at Yale, which I will tell you about in a minute, says its like the Enigma machine during World War II. They use the affinity to crack the code of the wider world. So what does it look like? We have got kids with all kinds of affinities showing their stuff on the Web site. That is one side of it.

The other side of it there is a team of neuroscientists that I am working with since the publication of the book, MIT, Yale, Simon Baron-Cohen at Cambridge University, folks at Duke, even some people at NIH because Tom Ensel is very psyched up about all of this. Here is what they are doing. They are bringing in communities of autistic spectrum kids at a young age. They are having them walk on to their affinity, and then they are doing the fMRI. Okay. Here he is in the sweet spot. Let's lighten up. Well, look at that. The reward circuitry is alight. Parts that deal with social cognition are firing. Actually this shows in this fMRI his compensatory skills because that is the key.

Again, you are an expert in neuroscience. You know we are living in the era of neuroscience. What have we learned just in the last 15 years since those terrible, terrible moments where the epileptic kids had to have half their brain taken out, and everyone said oh that is awful, and then they said, geez, the remaining half is doing everything both halves used to do, how is this working? We thought the brain was static. We thought if it doesn't happen by the time you are 3 years old, it ain't going to happen. We are born with more cells as a baby than any known thing in the universe, and we shake them and discard them until we die.

All of it wrong. We are constantly shaping our brains every day. You guys probably shaped it this morning frankly. We are growing cells and the brain is constantly improvising to find new neuro pathways. This is very hopeful because what do we find with our communities that the neuroscientists are affirming, a traditional pathway may be blocked, stressed by virtue of the hand they are dealt at birth. As they go out into the world and find their affinities, compensatory strengths are building.

It is just high school science, conservation of energy. It goes somewhere. Where is it going? That is what the researchers at MIT, Yale, and Cambridge are there to find out and once we begin to discover, which is the way this is moving now, and it is not just there, it is everywhere. Once we discover those compensatory muscles, we will start to say fine, I can nourish that. I can support that and that eventually is going to be something an employer says, oh, can I have one of them. Actually 100 of them would do.

What happens here? What happens is that we begin to tap enlightened self interest. Look, you all know as we all know, the only thing that works in a civil, free society in the free enterprise model, as the founding fathers knew, is enlightened self interest. We need to bring the enlightened here to the self interest, and we will do it working in unison.

Researchers, government, industry, and frankly folks like some of the folks at the panel here today who are pioneering new ways to see ourselves through this left-behind population. This is what always changes the arc of history, the moment where the left-behind population is seen as not them but us. That is where we are now.

So on the LifeAnimated.net site, we have neuroscientists looking at the videos of extraordinary feats of these kids who are discarded, and they are saying actually that is a neural pathway, and that is a neurological strength, and this is something an industry wants. That is one side of it.

Another side of it is we are setting up the affinity network where these affinities are going to be displayed and scaffolded, again with support, so that employers can say uh, there it is, and that is measured good. Can we have an exchange or conversation with that young adult. We will manage that conversation. They are not going to be out there in the swift winds of public without support. Again, these are things that government might get involved with. Just like ebay or Monster.com for special skills. The way the world works now, two.

Three, what I am now doing in the past 1½ months is meeting with folks out on the far and distant coast. Folks who are building augmentative technologies and creating a generation of augmentative technologies that will be exactly the kind supports that this population needs. There is no place in which the return on this investment will be greater, not just for the folks who want to jump in and invest, but more importantly for society at large because this is the era we are living in.

Now, Owen sees it as a side kick. He looks at Siri. He taps it on his iPhone. A couple months ago he says can I ask it anything. I said what would you ask it? And he starts reeling off what he would ask it. That helps him be context strong where he is often context blind. That is where we are going. This is something that is shared purpose, again not a zero sum game, a win-win. That is happening as part of a synergistic group of activities.

Let me just finish with this. These affinities create community. I am a kid and looking at the folks in the panel and all of you were kids. We are lumpy middle aged people or better, you couldn't find folks like you. Not so easy. You might have a club at high school, you might go to place where they did something like the comic shop or whatever it is. Well, now we can find each other. It is one of the great miracles of the connected age.

What is happening is that these affinities are forming communities and once that happens, these kids don't feel alone. They don't feel broken. They feel strength in numbers. And they are like we are all good at our thing. We are not less. This part we are more and this is what happens every week at Disney Club at my son's school. He started it when he got there 3 years ago, his college program at Cape Cod because he wanted friends. He wanted people like him.

What is fascinating and enlivening and hopeful is that many of the kids in Disney Club were not raised in this sort of crazy, ionized, animated character, affinity therapy workshop that our house became. They were raised just like most kids. Some of them were told cut off the affinity. It didn't vanish, and their passion did not diminish. When we get to Disney Club, it is like a dam break. The first Disney Club they are watching ''Dumbo.'' Great movie. Of course, Cornelia and I, my wife, we have been talking Disney for years. This is easy for us. We say to the kids, talk to me about ''Dumbo.'' Why is this a favorite? One of the young ladies says let me explain. This is a young girl who could not speak as a child. Many of the non-speaking kids bond with non-speaking characters early on that express all emotions without words. Why is that a surprise? She says well, you see the thing that made him different, his ears made him an outcast, and I understand that from my own life; but then he learned through his life that what made him different allowed him to soar.

This is the age we are in. This is a time where we can allow them to soar, and it will draw the best from us, not just as individuals, but as a society to say in this time we rose to the occasion of making the arc bent.

Thank you, Mr. Chairman.

[The prepared statement of Mr. Suskind follows:]

TESTIMONY OF RON SUSKIND

Pulitzer Prize-winning Journalist, author of "Life, Animated, A Story of Sidekicks, Heroes and Autism," and the senior fellow at Harvard's Center for Ethics.

HEARING ON

## The Global Autism Challenge

Before the United States House of Representatives

Committee on Foreign Affairs

Subcommittee on Africa, Global Health, Global Human Rights, and International Organizations

July 24, 2014

## Introduction

Thank you, Chairman Smith, Ranking Member Bass and Members of the Subcommittee. And thank you for this opportunity to discuss the global challenge autism presents and how we might respond to it, as engaged governments and citizens in the 21$^{st}$ century.

For the past 25 years, I've been writing about the ideals of public policy and the challenge of effective governance, education, race, and how we value – and reward – human capacity. As a journalist, predominantly at the Wall Street Journal, and in six books, I've attempted to understand how governments can do more, most effectively, for those in need.

A great deal of my work has focused on the left behind, here and abroad – from America's blighted urban core to Pakistan and Afghanistan, Europe and Africa. As I searched the world, seeking those separated from dignity and opportunity by poverty and by bigotry in their many forms, and documenting our era's scourge of tribalism supported by violence, I discovered that the most dramatically left-behind person I'd encountered was living in my own home.

That would be my son, Owen. Just before his third birthday, a chatting, playful boy was struck silent. Crying, inconsolable, he soon lost his few hundred-word, two-and-a-half year-old's vocabulary. By three, he was down to one word: "Juice." Soon enough, we received a diagnosis of regressive autism.

This story, of children trapped inside an unreachable world of autism, is all too common, for reasons we still don't understand, as today's distinguished guests and experts have so effectively described. The growth in diagnosed cases is startling, with three million in America and an estimated 70 million worldwide. The most bracing number from this year's CDC report is as follows: one out of 42 boys in the U.S. is on the autism spectrum. That's a rate of 2.5% of our male population.

I'm here today, though, to speak of hope. As a lifelong investigative reporter, I breathe skepticism. I am contrary by nature. I need proof, or I don't budge.

But what I'm finding now are outlines of a surprising and hopeful equation.

It starts with my family's own experience across 20 years of wrestling with my son's affinity. Virtually everyone on the autism spectrum has an affinity: a deep and special interest, a passion, that often appears to crest into obsession. That's the way most specialists have seen these affinities over recent decades, as perseverative, unproductive, a wheel in the ditch. The idea has long been to wean children off their affinity, even though that rarely works. My son's affinity is Disney animated movies. Don't worry, I won't start singing. Not yet, at least. From the earliest age, when he could not speak, we found he was memorizing the dialogue and song lyrics from his favorites – Dumbo, Pinocchio, the Lion King – by rewinding them over and over. Eventually we learned that he'd memorized about 20 of them – all the classics – and that if you threw him a line, he'd throw you back the next one. Of course, just about everything is found in the 55 Disney features since Snow White in 1937. We picked scenes – one for every occasion -- and began conversing in Disney dialogue. We became animated characters. Over years, this is how he got his speech back. He then created an interpretive, emotional language using Disney dialogue and, eventually, a powerful philosophy of life.

In other words, once we gently engaged his affinity, and began to exchange and share the fundamental emotions found in every family, he let us in deeper. Over a decade-plus, we realized he was using his affinity like the Enigma machine in WWII – to crack the codes of the wider world. We helped, certainly, as my wife worked with him round the clock, assisted by me, his older brother, Walt, and eventually teachers and therapists. But the key was the way his self-directed energies were channeled through his passion: he used Disney to broaden his knowledge of the real world, learn to read, widen his vocabulary, teach himself to draw masterfully and, most importantly, to manage his emotional growth.

We called it "Disney Therapy," and eventually skilled psychologists helped us hone it. Now, we call it "Affinity Therapy," because we've found there are many affinities – probably 20 major ones in this period, covering much of the ASD population – that growing evidence indicates can be used in the same way.

Thomas Insel, who heads the National Institute of Mental Health, calls affinity therapy a "reversal of the telescope," that may herald a new pathway to understand autism and help those with ASD. Since the publication of my book, neuroscientists at MIT, Yale and Cambridge University have joined to launch an international trial to study affinities. The protocol is to have children lock onto their affinity and, then using fMRI, seeing how their brains respond. The view – one affirmed by clinical observation – is that underlying neuronal capacities will be revealed. These capacities might be called the compensatory gifts of those with autism, evidence of how the brain, with its vast plasticity, finds a way; neural pathways – heavily weighted from birth or built because a traditional pathway is blocked – that can then be harnessed and nourished by therapists and educators.

Eventually, these will be the special skills and capacities tapped by employers.

Because that is our shared goal – finding productive lives for those with ASD. They want it, we want it. Society wants it. And, certainly, those who watch federal budgets want it.

How do we get there?

First, we must begin to change the way this population is viewed. More than half the ASD population is of normal or above-normal intelligence. With the difficulty in measuring their often subtle or shrouded abilities, and the deficits of using a one-size-fits-all yardstick for those with such specialized profiles, that percentage is surely higher. I would go further: as the neuroscientists at MIT and Yale secure funding and begin their trials, I would submit that for every visible deficit, there is an equal and opposing strength. This population is just like the rest of us, only less so and more so. The "less so" parts are conspicuous, and we focus on them intently, trying to fix them, to help them the individual be more like the blended average, and manage in the world. The "more so" parts are often subtle, opaque, hard to find and measure. But why is that a surprise – all our most important qualities are hard to measure. The question increasingly is not "if" these "more so" qualities exist, but "where?"

We're beginning to get answers displayed on the LifeAnimated.net website, where parents, therapists and those with ASD have recently posted videos of the often startling abilities housed in this population, each video showing how affinities are used to find a way into the sunlight of communication and human interaction. One parent I recently spoke with told me of how her nonspeaking son became fascinated with bees. The family pushed all available education – science, history, geography, math – through that fulcrum. The child's skills grew, as did his ability to connect to others. As a teenager, he secured a job at a bee-farm in California, using his deep knowledge. Until he typed out to his mother that it was no longer bees that fascinated him. . . it was now flowers. That's where his self-directedness then led. He is now an expert on flora and is working successfully at a large organic nursery, a star employee. Another child is an expert in wind chimes, showing more expertise than the leading maker of wind chimes in America (as demonstrated by a chime-identification contest between he and the company's CEO.) A third – a small boy – speaks through logos and commercial jingles, which he's memorized utterly. As parents, siblings, therapists and friends celebrate these affinities – the children are affirmed and respected. And emotionally deepened by that human contact, each one is progressing, on their way to become deeply specialized and expert adults.

Expertise – that's what businesses want. I have recently formed an Affinity Foundation, to act as a clearinghouse and data-sharing destination for research, as well as the beginnings of an affinity network, where special skills can be displayed and employers can shop for what they need: eBay meets Monster.com.

But, as my friend Thorkil Sonne has found, a valuable specialized skill is not enough, even if it can be identified and turned into an occupational path. ASD folks need social supports to manage in most workplaces. That's one place where funding can and should be focused: shoring up the bridges to traditional workplaces, allowing for sustainable and productive occupational engagements, or helping to create specialized workplaces where ASD achievers can work in a comfortable environment. Every public dollar spent here brings a return many times over.

One area of immediate need – and also federal support – is for a new generation of socially augmentative technology. In that regard, I've recently tapped the inventors of voice recognition technology and Siri, the personal assistant on your iPhone. Bringing them together with leading autism specialists, we're crafting a specialized app to fit the needs of ASD folks as they venture into the world. This app will be adaptable to fit an array of needs that are commonly shared in this community, but can be also be specialized by ASD individuals and their supporters – including job trainers and employers – to fit specific needs. The artificial intelligence functions will help the device get smarter and more supportive of each user. For years, my wife and I – experts on our son's needs and strengths and inclinations --dreamed of following him out the door each morning to school, to be a voice in is head, to remind him, reinforce behaviors, and give him the few prompts he'd need to get through the day. Now my son, at 23, knows the prompts that help him, the regular reminders and answered questions he needs to navigate the shifting terrain of daily life.

Soon, he'll have an app, which he can carry in his iPhone without stigma. Some people talk to themselves. My son's been doing that for years. Now, he can do it under his breath to his electronic "sidekick." Disney, as you know, has scores of sidekicks – Jiminy Cricket, Merlin, Rafiki. Owen often says the sidekick's job is to help the hero fulfill his destiny. This app will help with his hero's journey.

All together, these steps forward create that hopeful equation – hopeful, in that it fits with the way we know the world really works. We build skills and character through adversity, earn hard won insights, develop muscles, from walking into a strong headwind. I find this among "left behind" people throughout the world. What's changing in this connected age is that they're realizing this . . . and we, so often graced by opportunity and advantage, are realizing it. That's what, at day's end, binds my son to the many people I've reported about across the world; many of them unlettered and deeply disadvantaged, who have built powerful capacities to simply survive. Compensatory muscles? The greatest human trait is adaptability. We find a way to get what we need, to bend toward the sunlight.

What's coming next, or should be, is a validation of this basic human verity. There should be federal support for a new set of yardsticks to measure many forms of intelligence and capacity, rather than the gold-plated, one-size-fits-all yardsticks that now mostly reward the already advantaged or the traditional, generalized learner. Once these yardsticks are developed, educators and employers can more easily embrace the wide varieties of inclination and ability that is the underlying truth of human diversity. This incentive – enlightened self-interest – will drive change . . . change that, in the case of ASD folks, can be buoyed by the social supports and new generation of technologies to help them manage in the world. The bottom line: we cannot survive with so much human capacity, ability and passion being discarded. Unleashing the potential of vast "left behind" communities, including those with ASD other forms of neurological distinctiveness, is our only path forward.

And, with each passing day, the journey of my son – and countless folks like him – will get a touch easier, as people begin seeing him the way he increasingly sees himself: as not less, but different.

In the past few years, in his college program on Cape Cod, he's run Disney Club, where students of shared affinity gather each week to mediate over their favorites. Because they use this affinity as their form of communication, their expressive abilities are heightened, just as their identities are affirmed. A favorite, they all agree is Dumbo. Any one of these kids – all of whom have lived in life's discard pile – can explain why. The elephant was an outcast, because of his conspicuous difference – those giant ears – but he learned eventually that what made him different helped him soar. At a recent meeting, the members said they'd all learned that in their own lives – and discussed their "hidden ears." This trenchant insight puts them ahead of most of us, and society at large.

They're just waiting for the rest of us to catch up.

I thank the committee for its time and attention and would be glad to answer any questions.

———————

Mr. SMITH. Ron, thank you very much. That was an extraordinary bit of insight and sharing a personal history of you and your son Owen. Thank you so much for that.

You know, I think one of the bottom lines that you have shared with us is that best practices also include the yardstick, as you put it, how we look at and view those on the spectrum, and that is a change that hopefully happens not just in Washington, but across all of corporate America and then throughout the entire world, which is one of the reasons why we are launching this whole aging out issue.

Part of the CARES autism bill that has passed the House and is now pending in the Senate, is to get to the point of looking at what is available once you have aged out, housing, job opportunities, and we are hoping in at the end, all of your testimonies were just extraordinary. I still, and I have tried for a long time now, can't get USAID to focus on autism. So your testimonies will be put in writing to Dr. Shah who is a good man, who is the Administrator for USAID. CDC does some work overseas but not enough or any from USAID.

And your point, about the what you did, Mr. Rosanoff, in Ghana with the Health Minister from Tanzania and the First Lady of Ghana with 14 countries participating plus your work with Ethiopia. I had a hearing where we had women and children and families talk about what was available, and we had a woman from Cote D'Ivoire who talked about how in Cote d'Ivoire there was nothing available for her son, and she was one of the lucky ones at the time that went to Ohio and then received the full assistance of the state and municipality that she lived in.

So, again, your testimonies are great and I was in the Centro Ann Sullivan del Peru and saw, I mean, while we can share many best practices, we can also glean best practices from others, and I thought they had much to offer in Lima. It is a 30-year-old effort, and I was really impressed. I could tell you were too by your statement.

I would like to yield to my colleagues. I do have a couple questions, but I yield to Chaka Fattah.

And then go to my good friend from Pennsylvania.

Mr. FATTAH. Thank you, Mr. Chairman.

The World Health Organization indicates that there are well over 1 billion people worldwide suffering from one of some 600 brain-related diseases or disorders or challenges.

Autism is something that we have seen an increased prevalence of worldwide, and in our own country something like 1 out of 68 children are somewhere on this spectrum. We have got a gender situation where it is almost always a young boy, but I could just tell you the most hopeful thing I have heard is the testimony I just witnessed, Mr. Chairman.

And it is quite empowering. So, and Tom Ensel is someone who I deeply respect, and I know that the Institute has been quite focused on this issue, and I want to spend just a few minutes on this.

I had here on the Hill last week a young lady, Renee Gordon, whose son is an adult now and has had a whole set of challenges. But to jump to the positive, now he has got an iPhone that he can speak through. It hangs around his neck and to deal with the question of affinity, she had indicated that he knows every street in Washington, DC. You know, he can walk you through any museum. Because he has got this capacity, this strength, that others of us don't have in terms of this.

And it points to the work that you are doing around affinity. It is true that where every other description you would say that this young man was a low-functioning person, but in these particular areas, he functions beyond anyone else in terms of his ability. So there is something to be learned.

I spent some time at Boston University at the Autism Excellence Center, and I was taken by the art work done by young people, and there is so much that we can learn here and I think you really have flipped this on its head from looking at it in one way, to us looking at it in a much different way.

And so, Mr. Chairman, the other morning, on Tuesday I spent the morning at DARPA, and they are doing some great work on neuroscience, and a lot of people throughout our Government are doing important work and I just hope that as we look at this question about autism, that we put it in a broader context. I think about the gender bias. We see the same circumstances with schizophrenia. It is almost always a young male. And I am convinced that as we look at these things, that we are going to find solutions the broader we look and the deeper we look, and that is why the mapping of the brain and some of the other things that are not disease or disorder specific I think have an import in this effort because we have some real runway room here.

There is a lot for us to learn. We have learned a lot, but we have to do more and we have to do it from a global perspective. And you know, the EU's efforts, Henry Markram, the efforts in Israel with the Israeli brain technology, all around the world people working and that is why I am glad as chair of the committee you have taken this on to kind of look at it from a global context.

So I thank you, and I thank you for all of your testimony. I read it before. We were over on the floor, so I wanted to jump the gun before you—I didn't know you hadn't testified.

But thank you very much. Thank you.

Mr. SUSKIND. You have inspired me, sir. Thank you.

Mr. SMITH. Mr. Meehan.

Mr. MEEHAN. Well thank you, Mr. Chairman.

And I think all of you inspire us as well with not only your—your persistence. You know and I think that is the kind of thing, I have the joy of living next to a neighbor with a young child, and we have the joy of watching him grow, but I have watched the parents, too and it is a remarkable thing to see. I know it is not always easy, but working not just to survive but to develop these into this next place is really what I think is so special about this hearing.

Let me start first. And I am struck by, Mr. Suskind, your talks about the affinities and the identification of places, but Mr. Velasco, you have similarly used that same language, and if you could talk about your experience where you discussed the idea that so often those who have autism and have a lot of other coping capacities and skills to bring never get through the first interview, once they disclose something, and so they are constantly in the same vein in which you have identified it, seem to be ready to go and then they get knocked down by us.

And yet here you are, taking the time to say, wait a second. Let us find this affinity, and, in fact, you are finding workers that in many ways are superior and that is sort of a breakthrough if only we are able to channel this understanding and have others begin to appreciate the opportunity that exists and is very special.

So would you share with me your experiences, whether this experiment has met your expectations or perhaps even exceeded them, and I am particularly interested in how you focus on that particular strength that you are able to develop?

Mr. VELASCO. Absolutely and thank you for the opportunity to share once more our experience with the Autism at Work program.

George Brown is one of our new employees. George is early 40s in age, and he allowed me to share his experiences with you and with this panel and members of the audience. Just yesterday he sent me an email, and he said for many years I went through the interview process only to be rejected over and over again. I would take this skill or that skill that they asked me to learn. I would take or acquire this certification or that certification that they asked me to acquire to be marketable and employable. I went through college because they told me I needed a college degree; and at the end, he said, I was still being rejected. I suffer, he said, from deep depression because I continue to be rejected.

What I find in Mr. Brown is a tremendous resiliency, of course, because he has been through this for many, many years. I found this passion for the work he does at SAP to be inspiring to other people. His testimony as a worker I think is unparalleled. He is as involved as any of the other 12 new colleagues that we have here at SAP. Does he have the capabilities that we are looking for? Absolutely. George has a degree in business administration with a specialization in management of information systems. So from purely a skill perspective, he has what we need in the organization, aligned with the emphasis, of course, that we are seeing in his day-to-day activities with the company.

We also have other people like Janis Oberman. Janis is 56 years old, and Janis was unemployed from the year 2000 until 2014 approximately. She has a master's degree, and she has an undergraduate degree from the University of California at Berkeley. She was diagnosed with autism late in her age. She is a software tester, quality assurance in the business products that we sell to our customers.

And what we are finding is that again the capabilities are there, the ability is there, the desire to work is there, but it is just that the other side of the table sometimes doesn't have the capability to understand and harvest that talent. I believe that as organizations start maturing and learning that there is this pervasive skill out in the market, and as we start seeing that there is an enormous amount of job openings out there in science, technology, engineering, and mathematics, that if something is not working right when you find that there is people that are unemployed, underemployed or partially employed who deserve a better shot.

Our expectation at SAP is that those capabilities that we are seeing at work right now will pay off in the long term, in the short term as well, but in the long-term in retention practices as well as, because the cost associated for companies like ours to replace an employee go as much as 150 percent of the annual salary of the person being replaced. Now, if you have an attrition rate or a turn-over rate in a company of 10 to 15 percent, which is typical in many software companies, replacement costs are a huge loss of money for the organization. So we are seeing that not only the skill acquisition, but also the retention of employees as something of extreme value.

And so far what we are seeing in our employees again is thatresiliency, that intense desire to work, to come up to work every day and contribute as being you know, an enormous driver and inspiration for the rest of us in the organization.

Mr. MEEHAN. I thank you for that commitment, and I hope that you will, as you further unlock this secret and build the record for these successes, that you won't be worried that your colleagues at some of these other technology companies will catch up with you, that you will take that information and allow it to be shared so that others won't be afraid to explore the possibilities and develop the potential.

And I think, Mr. Suskind, you really developed this concept in the testimony which I found so intriguing. And I had an experi-ence, Garnet Valley High School in my area is working in a very proactive way working with really two groups, which is kind of neat. The juniors and seniors are being taught robotics and how do the process of manufacturing and operation. The children in the grammar school, I watched the robot, and it sits and speaks and talks to them and the teacher said that.

You know, when I talk to them, you can see the seven children around, and the engagement was, they knew the  teacher,  they were comfortable. There was a little more action with us in the room, but there was a sort of the management of the orchestra that was still warming up. But when they put the robot on, the children just came in, and they engaged in a way that I had never seen be-fore, and they were sort of enjoying this concept that they are breaking through to something. Seems to me they are on to this concept that you were discussing.

Tell me a little bit more about how we discover this in more ways, and certainly we know about the spectrum. There is really remarkably talented folks with a few issues, and there are some that are really struggling, as you said, to even say a word or tie a shoe. Do we find that same possibility on the full spectrum?

Mr. SUSKIND. We do. We do. It is interesting because I arrived at this, Congressman, with what I say the same usual set of neurotypical prejudices and blind spots. I don't even know what the word neurotypical means anymore. Frankly this whole experience has helped me look at myself and people I know with new eyes.

We are probably all, in some years hence this will be discovered, we are probably all a mixture of many spectrums, many bands of color in the human rainbow. We have concentrations here and you know, less concentrations there. I think that's the reality that we are all now seeing in some ways for the first time.

What you are seeing now though are people recognizing  that many of the ways we measure human capacity, i.e., expressive speech, well, it doesn't track with underlying cognition. I know many, many kids with inabilities. We got 40 percent of the folks on the autism spectrum have little or no speech. They have now a new buffet, but they need more frankly here of augmentative devices, where they type. I have a friend whose son types 180 words a minute quite beautifully, grammatically perfect. The kid's got real talent. He cannot talk to you. But what he is doing is he processing the world again through his powerful muscle, his Enigma machine, and he is breaking codes every day.

Part of what you find though, what you are talking about, this robot, is that what I think many of the researchers have found, is that when there is something that is a verisimilitude of reality but a little off to the side, which is a little bit what this community does, they create an alternative alongside reality that kind of works, it grabs them. It draws them in.

I mean, right now, and you can go online and see this, someone I know up at MIT, Cynthia Breazeal, who is the robotics chief up the MIT has created this robot, Jibo. And this thing is a desktop robot that does very much what you are talking about, and it is quite enlivening. And you can see how it draws in neurotypical people, but for the spectrum community, this could be a pathway to joy.

I mean for instance, I can see Owen. Owen and I watched Cynthia's video not too long ago, and he is like, wow, so I could have the robot do all kinds of stuff. I said yeah. I could have it play a video? Uh-huh. And I could talk to it? Well, we can't do that. That is another company, ToyTalk where you can talk to the video and it talks back. I mean this is where we are going. We are all becoming kind of a version of Cyborg here. We are all augmented by a new generation of technologies.

And what is interesting is that it goes not just to this community but how this community is a canary in the coal mine showing us ourselves more clearly as to what the future might look like. This is where enlightened self interest gets involved. You know, in some ways they are the R&D lab for what will be working for the rest of us. It is not just the app we're building. Everyone is going to want the app because, look, I can use that, too. Developing context as I walk through the world. It is more than that.

It is that the neuroscientists, as the Congressman understands, and anyone who deals with neuroscience is that Eric Kandel says it best. Understanding autism means we will understand the human brain. Why? Because it is odd and fascinating in the way it opens a window to seeing the brain in its more so and less so concentrations. So that means not just the areas that are challenged. That means neuroscientists saying look at the more so parts. Can my brain do that? That is where we see possible futures, where this community will start to lead. This is the sweet spot.

And, part of what we could do together is to support the programs that alter perspectives and the framing of the debate. I mean, once that happens, much of this will carry itself forward, but that is kind of where we are right now. It is to say how can I help people see what the underlying science shows and what many people on the panel here know from long, hard-earned experience.

Once that happens, this room grows. This table multiplies, and people start saying this is not about them, because they are us. This is about how through them, we all move forward and we are all better off. That is where a change occurs.

Mr. MEEHAN. Mr. Chairman, thank you for the courtesy of being able to be with you here with you today, and I really want to thank the panel for their tremendous and uplifting testimony.

I am inspired and I am very grateful for the work that the constituent company has been doing at SAP. I look forward to continuing to work with you on these possibilities.

I have a thing I am late for, but I thank you for the chance to participate.

Mr. SMITH. I will just ask a few final questions, and again your testimonies will be disseminated very widely as soon as we get the full record together, so thank you for that.

And, your points have been brilliant. I think you have focused on different things. I think the idea of looking at this you know, from a way we have not done before is greatly required to move forward and to make advancements. Talking about enlightened self interest, how do we go about getting the CEOs, the hiring specialists in companies, to really recognize, you know, the jewel that awaits them if they hire a person on the spectrum?

Mr. VELASCO. Congressman Meehan had a really good point, and that was precisely in that direction. How do we make it happen? And I think that sharing is a key element of that.

What we have done at SAP is we have opened up a number of venues for other employees to come and visit with us. We share what we have the minute that we have it available, so as soon as we are wrapping up our pilot programs, we are in a position to share our learnings. We have had up to now approximately 15 companies who have approached us, very large companies, very committed companies. One of them just told us last week that they had received final approval for their own Autism at Work program.

Mr. SMITH. Are you at liberty to say who they are?

Mr. VELASCO. Yes. The name is Capital One.

Mr. SMITH. Thank you.

Mr. VELASCO. Thank you.

Mr. SMITH. You know, if I could, while you are answering that question, maybe you could elaborate, too, a little bit being from Denmark and with your European background, on how the Europeans are doing on this.

And another question for you all, and Ms. Hussman, you might to want to touch on this as well. If 50,000 autistic American children are matriculating into adulthood every year, what are the numbers around the world? Are they along the same demographic, or has it lagged or what in other parts of the world, and how many do we see, you know, of the 70 million, how many of those are becoming adults?

Mr. SONNE. Well, I have 10 years of experience from Denmark and we still have employees with autism working at the first couple of clients we have in Denmark, so it says something about retention and resilience.

And what I experience here in the U.S. is that there is huge interest in focusing on talents here. I relocated to Delaware because

Governor Markell said, I will get the stakeholders together. We have a lot of high tech jobs that are vacant and we have more and more people being diagnosed. So he chaired the meetings and showed political leadership that now has resulted in Delaware being our base for the U.S. What it takes is for the corporate sector to really request these people, because we have to turn from a push to a pull.

We have to have companies like SAP doing the storytelling, but Specialisterne is also a case study at Harvard business school because we manage what they call the outliers, and they claim that the winners in a global knowledge-based market economy will be the companies who are at best at managing outliers because the edge is where innovation comes from.

And in the latest issue of MIT Sloan Management Review, there is a story about the dandelion philosophy of how to see always the herb angle instead of the weed angle so you see a dandelion, and this is also what we have been discussing here today. Instead of looking at the deficits, let's park that, and let's see the strengths.

I think that time is on our side because there are so many vacant jobs in this STEM sector, in the high tech sector, and thanks to stories from companies like SAP, we can get the companies to really say, wow, we missed something here. Let's follow the SAP example. But there are also many with autism who do not qualify for the high tech jobs. But then there is the 503, the new rule saying that 7 percent of people with disabilities should be working for you if you want Federal tasks.

So that can really broaden the spectrum, not just for the high end part of the spectrum, but we can really have the opportunity to make Janis and George show the way, open the doors from the companies and then get as much talent in play among people with autism and similar challenges. There are many others who have challenges similar to autism, and we have to remember them, and hopefully we can get people with autism to open the door for people who have other challenges but have a lot of talent and capacity if the employers will accommodate for that.

And I really follow Ron's example of the canary in the mine shaft, because I claim that a workplace where our people thrive will be a good place to work for everyone.

Mr. SMITH. Ms. Hussman, I thought your testimony was excellent, but your point that the lack of our Nation's attention to fully integrate those living with autism into mainstream society, and you make a very important point which was created frankly by the ADA. Through universal access is often expected of buildings and stairways, our society has yet to build universal accesses into schools curricula, workplaces, our hearts, or our minds. If you can again answer the original question, but I think that point was very well taken.

Ms. HUSSMAN. Yes. So one of my concerns in the dialogue here, or my experience in the dialogue here, is Mr. Suskind gave the percentage of 40 percentage are non-verbal or partially verbal, and so when we talk about the high skill jobs, we need to be coming at this from both—actually the logistics of the table works out well, from both ends.

What you will notice in many of the stories is that it took time, patience and support from many of the positive stories that you are hearing, and a lot of hours of a lot of parents and what we need is to shift that, not just from the parents, but to society as a whole when we talk about changing our minds and making the ADA bigger than our stairways and our doorways, is to say that our teachers, you have to pick special ed to get any training on autism or anything else. But I would defy you to walk into any American classroom today and not find someone with a learning disability, someone on the spectrum, somebody who needs different supports.

So our curricula for our teachers alone could significantly change the landscape of people's perceptions when somebody comes to you for a job or somebody comes to you for some other opportunity or tries out for a team. So I am not sure that I answered your question but——

Mr. SMITH. Before you go, the worldwide demographic, again moving into the adulthood stage, is it pretty much universal around the globe, or is it just——

Mr. ROSANOFF. So, Mr. Congressman, I can offer some comment there about numbers. Really the 50,000 children transitioning to adulthood each year is a number that is derived from the U.S. prevalence estimate of about 1 percent. We need to keep in mind that that prevalence estimate is among children. Our best estimates of prevalence around the world are about the same, around 1 percent, so yes, we can think about it in terms of similar numbers. I can tell you from you know, experience in meeting with families around the world that this aging out issue, this transition to adulthood issue, is a major one and one that is on many people's minds.

But the point I want to come back to and I think the important point we shouldn't forget is that we really don't know how many adults there are with autism in the United States and around the world. Again the prevalence estimates are based on children. We have an estimate that about 1 percent of adults have autism and if that's the case, then there are more adults today with autism than children with autism. But I think it is important to remember that many of these adults may not have formal diagnoses. They may be in different sectors of society. Some may be comfortable and contributing to society but with challenges that I think could benefit from more attention given to these individuals.

We need to, I think, keep that in mind. When structuring these programs, an individual may not necessarily have to have the diagnosis with the consideration that they may have autism and just may not have a diagnosis yet. So improving our ability to identify adults with autism will help us better help them overcome their challenges and again find those opportunities to contribute to society.

Mr. SMITH. Briefly, in your testimony you talked about 14 African nations that you were a part of and the First Lady of Ghana and the Health Minister of Tanzania. What has come of that? Did they come up with an action plan? Was there a follow-up to it?

Mr. ROSANOFF. This was really a first of its kind type of meeting where the idea was to bring together advocates and various stakeholders from African countries, to share their experiences. This was an opportunity to demonstrate that there are similar challenges across countries, and even though there may be differences in culture and resources, there are common challenges that then allow for common opportunities to work together to collaborate and to develop these types of solutions.

So really this was a first chance for various groups around the African continent to come together and think about an African autism network where the idea would be to develop strategies to raise awareness of autism across the continent but also build capacity for services and research.

Mr. SMITH. Mr. Sonne, you had mentioned autism in Africa in your testimony and mentioned Nigeria has one adult psychiatrist serving the needs over 1 million people and the disproportionality of specialists and professionals to the number of people who are affected. I am working on a case now with CURE where they are trying to help children with hydrocephalus, especially those who get it from an infection base, and they have cured 5,000 kids in Uganda through a simple non-shunt related, no shunts are needed, and I went there and watched it. So did Greg and we actually one of the trained neurosurgeons come over and testified. He did it by Skype, so we saw him over there, and the idea is to build out a capacity of 100 neurosurgeons over time.

We were also trying to get USAID to focus on that and thus far have failed miserably. But that said, it seems to be there is a similar type of lack of capacity and if you don't have the skilled personnel you could have absolutely committed parents, but they also need that specialist's insight and diagnosis in the first place. What are your thoughts on that?

Mr. SONNE. Well I think, it is a matter of making the pull from the companies in Nigeria and other African countries, then I am sure that companies like SAP, they know what they are looking for and as we discussed, there are many adults with autism, probably the majority, who do not have a diagnosis but have the same traits and have the same talents that the companies are looking for.

And I think when companies have learned from our experiences and SAP's leadership here, they will create environments where people with autism thrive, but also people who are not diagnosed with autism will thrive and I think that will be a magnet. I think it will be known in the community. Well, you will know if you have challenges in social interactions and teamwork, but you are really good at math, physics, IT, chess player, type, so you would know that SAP, for example, would be a good place to go for you to work.

My ultimate goal is really where we can take autism out of our equation and say this is not just about autism. This is about good management, and this is about giving companies access to talent and to help the companies find that talent and describe the shape it comes in.

And many will have a diagnosis. Many will not. But I think if the needs, if the pull is there from the companies, if we can apparently empower the society and the families to learn social entrepreneurship, work with stakeholders, then you will not need an autism diagnosis in order to get in to thrive in program like at SAP.

Mr. SMITH. Let me just ask maybe SAP or either you could answer this or anyone. A large number of people get jobs first as interns. My legislative director, Cate Benedetti, just walked in. She first started as an intern. We got to know her, got to see her work product. Then Mary Noonan, our chief of staff, decided to hire her. Is there any kind of consideration given to SAP or in this model that would bring in some of the students before they cross over to adulthood?

Mr. VELASCO. This is an incredibly important topic. The issue of transitions, and transitions happen all the way from high school to college, and for those who go through college to professional life. One of the things that we see is that people in the spectrum after they graduate from college, the ones that are able to finish, a junior college or a college degree, oftentimes drop and they have a 2- or 3-year cliff you know, where they are unemployed, and this is where they start asking themselves why can't I find a position, a job. There is something wrong with me. Right.

So it impacts people quite a bit. What we are doing right now is exploring the possibility of an internship platform at the company, allowing people to come in, in the junior year. This is still on the design phase, but it is something that we have our eyes set on. We believe we need to capture talent early on before they graduate, people with a degree, sort of education that we are looking for, and the idea is that we will introduce this process hopefully within next year.

Mr. SONNE. Yes, what we are doing right now is we are working with this assessment, training and on boarding model. We are building bridges between people with autism and companies like SAP. But we want to remove the divide, and we can do that if we can work with the education system and the companies to have more crossover, to have the role models from the companies being involved in the school system and to have the students in internships.

We have a youth education in Denmark where we do a lot of that. They are in internships at our corporate partners. We teach life skills as well because this is more important than what we are doing now. If we can work with the education system, we will hopefully be able to remove the divide and inspire by new way of seeking talents and to teach the companies new ways of management. Then we can remove the divide that is there today.

Mr. SMITH. Mr. Suskind, final word.

Mr. SUSKIND. It is interesting. You talk about these models of in a way exposure. There is lots of suspicion and confusion, and then they sit with the spectrum kid, the young adult, and they are like, huh, not what I thought. That is what the internship platforms are doing. You guys are leading that charge. That is something that should be happening everywhere. Every kid these days starts with an internship. No one is getting paid before they are 24. So that is an opportunity for these kids to not be different also being interns. That is one thing.

The second thing that I felt was interesting a minute ago when you were talking about models that work in Africa, is that I am an old enough guy that I remember talk of the new Federalism back when, that states would be labs for programs, and the Federal Government would pass it to the states to figure out what works best. Well, now we are in a global experimental model that countries that lead here will be demonstration models for what works, and you may find a surprise as to some countries that you would not expect to be leading that take the lead.

I consider this when I think of incentives which is much of what we talked about today, a kind of incentive for a country maybe in Africa who gets put way down the list of possibility, says we have been able to shape something that can be used as a model for others. You know, a big challenge here that we have talked about in a different way all day, is something that I deal with at Harvard when I talk about narrative. It is about reframing the narrative. We all make sense of our world and ourselves through stories. Our kids, of course, do it very dramatically.

And we talk about a lot of the math science kids that, of course, you guys have embraced. I am spending time with TED talks for the humanities types, lots of kids who work and live inside of stories and develop stories. Well, they get this, they get this in ways that even we don't. That is a big part of what is so positive about this. Again, extreme versions of us that often reveal our capacities back to ourselves. That is a golden point here and in this case, they make sense of their life and their world through story.

And the story here is reshaping, but it needs to be reshaped with a kind of solidity of purpose to give the employers the yardsticks, the tools they need, so they have no excuse. I have got the data now, okay, I have got this yardstick which measures this array, this buffet of compensatory skills. Now I have no excuse and in fact, I now have what you talked about, Thorkil, before; I have comfort in my corporate thinking where I want to reduce risk and I want to optimize potential and profit. That is the way companies think.

Well, when they get those yardsticks to show capacity, again in this wide range, this arc of many types of intelligence, it gives them comfort on the risk side. It also gives them hope on the profit side. That is the only thing that will work here, and part of what we can do here is give them the tools, the supports, so that those corporate decisions will be the decisions that ultimately carry forward, not just the individual good, but the wider self interest of society, and I think it is within reach.

Ms. HUSSMAN. Chairman, if I could, back on the numbers in other countries, we are in two cases, we have some schools in Asia, in Thailand and Burma, and we also have a grant with the Carter Center in Liberia where they are specifically addressing mental health as an umbrella and the approach is to educate, the further out you get from urban areas, it is just that. It is just an umbrella of mental health. If you have epilepsy, they believe you are mentally ill, and you will be chained until you work through your seizures.

And so when we talk about the numbers, I think that until we get to a place of education, that there are specific disorders underneath of it, and in Asia we are finding, actually we sent our son, and there too, you have found that it is just, in the society that is so tough just to get through the day, that there is just a label of a mental disorder and our son was able to say no, I think he has autism, because he is familiar with it.

And if I could just make one other point for the day is that when we talk about the 40 percent non-verbal, when we talk about the progress and the skills, that it is not always just an economic benefit that these kids bring to our society.

And so, that is the whole spectrum that we are talking about, that sometimes just bringing a society's ability to recognize the value in ourselves at a better level, it has got some economic benefit to it as well, even if they are not——

Mr. SUSKIND. Creates a more humane civilization, doesn't it?

Ms. HUSSMAN. Yes. Yes.

Mr. SMITH. Beautifully put.

Unfortunately there is a vote on and it is at zero, so I am going to have to dart off.

Thank you so much. This is part a of series. We have had other hearings on global autism, but this one has a very specific focus on the aging out issue.

And all of your testimonies were extraordinary and I think will enlighten the Congress. It certainly enlightened me. Thank you.

[Whereupon, at 5:17 p.m., the subcommittee was adjourned.]

# APPENDIX

MATERIAL SUBMITTED FOR THE RECORD

# SUBCOMMITTEE HEARING NOTICE
# COMMITTEE ON FOREIGN AFFAIRS
## U.S. HOUSE OF REPRESENTATIVES
## WASHINGTON, DC 20515-6128

### Subcommittee on Africa, Global Health, Global Human Rights, and International Organizations
### Christopher H. Smith (R-NJ), Chairman

July 24, 2014

### TO:  MEMBERS OF THE COMMITTEE ON FOREIGN AFFAIRS

You are respectfully requested to attend an OPEN hearing of the Committee on Foreign Affairs, to be held by the Subcommittee on Africa, Global Health, Global Human Rights, and International Organizations in Room 2200 of the Rayburn House Office Building (and available live on the Committee website at www.foreignaffairs.house.gov):

**DATE:**       Thursday, July 24, 2014

**TIME:**       2:00 p.m.

**SUBJECT:**       The Global Challenge of Autism

**WITNESSES:**       Mr. Jose H. Velasco
Vice President of Product Management and Head of Autism at Work Initiative
SAP

Mr. Thorkil Sonne
Founder and Chairman
Specialisterne

Ms. Theresa Hussman
Board Member
Autism Society

Mr. Michael Rosanoff
Associate Director, Public Health Research
Autism Speaks

Mr. Ron Suskind
Author

### By Direction of the Chairman

*The Committee on Foreign Affairs seeks to make its facilities accessible to persons with disabilities. If you are in need of special accommodations, please call 202/225-5021 at least four business days in advance of the event, whenever practicable. Questions with regard to special accommodations in general (including availability of Committee materials in alternative formats and assistive listening devices) may be directed to the Committee.*

# COMMITTEE ON FOREIGN AFFAIRS

MINUTES OF SUBCOMMITTEE ON _Africa, Global Health, Global Human Rights, and International Organizations_ HEARING

Day__ _Thursday___ Date_____ _July 24, 2014_____ Room_ _2200 Rayburn HOB_

Starting Time ___ _2:08 p.m.___ Ending Time ___ _5:15 p.m._

Recesses |__ _1_ __| ( _2:46_ to _3:54_ ) (___to___) (___to___) (___to___) (___to___) (___to___)

---

**Presiding Member(s)**

_Rep. Chris Smith_

---

_Check all of the following that apply:_

Open Session [✓]                          Electronically Recorded (taped) [✓]
Executive (closed) Session [ ]            Stenographic Record [✓]
Televised [✓]

---

**TITLE OF HEARING:**

_The Challenge of Global Autism_

---

**SUBCOMMITTEE MEMBERS PRESENT:**

_Rep. Mark Meadows_

---

**NON-SUBCOMMITTEE MEMBERS PRESENT:** _(Mark with an * if they are not members of full committee.)_

_Rep. Patrick Meehan, Rep. Chaka Fattah_

---

**HEARING WITNESSES: Same as meeting notice attached? Yes [✓] No [ ]**
_(If "no", please list below and include title, agency, department, or organization.)_

---

**STATEMENTS FOR THE RECORD:** _(List any statements submitted for the record.)_

---

TIME SCHEDULED TO RECONVENE _____
or
TIME ADJOURNED ___ _5:15 p.m._

_Gregory B. Simpkins_
**Subcommittee Staff Director**